FIRST, A PROMISE

I promise you: Next time you give a talk or teach a lesson, if you follow three simple principles David O. McKay shared in 1905, you'll enhance the lives of everyone who listens to you — and your own life. The principles are:

1. HAVE AN OBJECTIVE
2. USE EXAMPLES
3. EMPHASIZE APPLICATION

If those three ideas are all you take away from this book — in fact, if you don't buy it; if you're just scrolling through the first pages or skimming it in a bookstore — the promise still applies: Those seven words will improve your talks, reduce your anxiety, and help you preach the gospel effectively.

For extra credit, check out the advice in chapter 5, too.

Richard Nash
Salt Lake City
September 2022

PRAISE FOR 3 KEYS...
AND HOW THE KEYS WILL HELP YOU

"If you're anxious before a talk, this book is spiritual Pepto Bismol."

— *Jeni Jones, a Primary teacher who doesn't much like public speaking*

"Give a copy to your high councilman. President McKay's advice really works!"

— *H. Gary Pehrson, former president, Connecticut Hartford Mission*

"*3 Keys to Help You Give a Better Talk* is just like the talks it teaches readers to give: direct, succinct, substantive, full of personal and historical examples, and memorable. While I was reading the book, I actually found myself wishing for a member of the bishopric to call me with a speaking assignment!"

— *Emily Wirthlin, returned missionary and BYU student*

"These are the right three principles. When we use these principles, people not only understand us, they can't misunderstand us. Simplicity on this side of complexity is not a great value, but simplicity on the other side of complexity is worth everything. This book is on the other side of complexity."

— *Greg McKeown, bishop and author of Essentialism*

"This book is just like a great talk — it's brief, it's filled with stories, and parts of it are funny. The advice about telling stories and how to find the right stories is especially inspired. People of all ages love stories. We often remember them more than any other part of a talk!"

— *Blair M. Kent, stake president*

3 KEYS
TO HELP YOU GIVE
A BETTER TALK

3

KEYS

TO HELP YOU GIVE
A BETTER TALK

SIMPLE, SOOTHING ADVICE
FROM DAVID O. MCKAY

RICHARD NASH

To Laurie
Always to Laurie

CONTENTS

INTRODUCTION TO DAVID O. MCKAY'S
THREE PRINCIPLES

Two things happened before I taught a Primary class in the fall of 2015: First, I had an impression that the lesson would go well — the Spirit would be there. And second, the kids in the class didn't have that impression.

Of the five kids, two were scoundrels — bickering and arguing with each other and with me. Two were bored; looking at the ceiling, just waiting for the lesson to end. One was an angel, listening and attentive. They were 10 and 11, old enough to understand what we were talking about, which was Jesus's role in guiding our lives, and old enough to behave better than they were behaving.

As the lesson dragged on, I remembered what I used to say when my kids were teenagers: *Next time I get a vote, I'm voting "no" on free agency.*

But I kept lurching through the lesson, and 80 percent of the kids kept being either antagonistic or disengaged. We had an activity. I used a visual aid. The misery continued. I asked a question: *Have you had an experience where you've felt the Lord was directing you?* I looked from one class member to the next. The answer was: *Yeah, kind of.*

I said: *Can you tell me about it?* I called on two of the kids by name. Their answers: *Well, you know, you just do what you think you should.*

I looked at my notes. I said: *Let me tell you two stories about how the Lord can direct you.*

I said: When I was a bishop, I was struck with a thought about a member of our ward who didn't come to church. I'd run into her and had a brief conversation the previous week, and on Sunday morning in bishopric meeting I said: We need to give this sister a calling. So we thought about an assignment for her, said a prayer to seek the Lord's blessing, and arranged a visit.

A couple of days later one of my counselors and I dropped by her home. She invited us in, she was sweet and gracious, and after a short conversation I said: Sister So-and-So, we have a calling we feel impressed to extend — we'd like you to do… whatever the calling was. I can't remember what we asked her to do.

But I remember the sister's reaction. She didn't say anything. She started to cry. She held her face in her hands for a moment, then looked up and said: Bishop, I've known I've needed to come back to church, but I've been afraid, so I've been praying I could get a calling. I knew a calling would make it easier for me to come back. So, yes, I'll accept the calling.

I finished the story and looked at the five faces in our Primary classroom. Only one — our class's angel — was looking back at me. The feeling among the rest was: *Yeah, well, bishops do stuff like that.* We'd turned a corner, but the lesson wasn't on track — yet.

So I said: Let me tell you another story. I said: This is about a time I felt the Lord's direction and didn't follow it. I was very young, maybe six or seven. My parents had gone out for the evening and left my brothers and me with a babysitter. And my older brother, Mike, who was three years older than I was, did something that really bugged me, and he did it enough to really make me mad. I remember trying to hit him, but our babysitter was right there, and he stepped behind her — and I faced them in our dining room, me on one side of the room, our babysitter on the other side, and Mike behind her. I picked up a container of crayons that was on the table; I remember it was an old cottage cheese carton, filled with crayons of all colors, and I lifted it so I could throw it.

The babysitter said: *Richard, put the crayons down.*

And I remember thinking: *I ought to put them down.*

But Mike, behind the babysitter, looked out at me, and he didn't stick out his tongue and waggle his fingers in his ears, but he had an expression on his face that said he was thinking about it. It was like: Hah. You're stuck. Neener-neener.

I stretched my arm back and aimed the crayons.

And again, the babysitter said: *Richard — DON'T throw those crayons.*

And again, I remember feeling, very clearly: *She's right. I shouldn't throw them.*

And Mike, behind the babysitter, grinned again in an especially infuriating way.

So I threw the crayons at him as hard as a little kid could.

I missed. I hit the babysitter. Mike had ducked completely behind her. Some of the crayons hit her and some shotgunned all over the room. She was upset. She didn't spank me, didn't even grab me, but she chewed me out, and I had to pick up the crayons, then I had to apologize to her, and to Mike.

Then, when my parents got home, she told them what had happened, and I got in trouble all over again.

Something started to happen as I told the story in Primary. The Spirit didn't join us, but the kids who'd been bickering gave up their squabble. The kids who'd been bored sat up in their chairs. They listened. There was a degree of attentiveness in our small classroom that started to solidify into reverence. Then I said: *I remember feeling very clearly that I shouldn't throw the crayons — and I know that during your life, you'll sense the Lord directing you. I know, and bear testimony: When you follow that direction, when you do what the Lord wants you to do, you'll be happy.*

And then the impression I'd had before the lesson was fulfilled. The Spirit was there. Much of the lesson wasn't very good; a lot of it never quite got on track. But years later, the kids told me they still remember that story, and I hope they'll remember the lesson I learned over 50 years ago: When you feel like you ought to do something, no matter how mad you are at your brother, don't throw the crayons.

AN EXAMPLE: HOW 'PREACHING OF THE WORD' CAN CHANGE LIVES

I love what Alma says in Alma 31:5: "The preaching of the word had a great tendency to lead the people to do that which was just — yea, it had had more powerful effect upon the minds of the people than the sword, or anything else, which had happened unto them." I've seen that powerful effect numerous times as a teacher and a student — and I was touched by it when I first read *Spiritual Roots of Human Relations* by Stephen Covey when I was a young man.

Brother Covey told the story of speaking to a group of fraternity/sorority students in a sorority house at the University of Arizona in the 1960s. His topic was "The new morality." He said:

The house was packed with about 150 young people. They were sitting in the front room, in the dining room, in the hallway, and up the stairs. I had a terrific sense of being overwhelmed and surrounded, and I felt very alone.

The new morality is a situational ethic based on the idea that there are no absolute truths and standards, but that each situation must be looked at in terms of the people involved as well as other factors that might be present. I put forth my view and my conviction that there is a God, that there are absolute truths and standards that have been revealed, and that the new morality is merely a rationalized old immorality. I sensed throughout my entire presentation considerable resistance and disbelief. When it came to the question and answer period, two articulate students began to express themselves strongly in favor of this situational ethic of the new morality. One was particularly effective and persuasive and acknowledged to the entire group that he knew it would be wrong for young people who were unmarried to live together as man and wife; he said he wasn't advocating any evil thing, but that love is so sacred and so beautiful, if an unmarried man and woman truly and deeply loved each other enough, then a premarital relationship would be logical and right.

Brother Covey continued to make a case for traditional morality; he quoted some scriptures to support his argument, but they weren't well-received. He talked about the heartbreak that resulted from breaking the law of chastity, but he sensed he was losing his audience. "To many of these students I was pretty much out of it," he said. He continues his story:

I remembered praying inwardly for some help and direction, and I came to feel that I should teach the idea of listening to the still, small voice of the Lord, of their conscience. I quoted the scripture earlier mentioned, Revelation 3, and indicated that if they would listen very carefully, they would hear a voice. It wouldn't be audible, and they wouldn't hear it in their ear, but they would hear it or feel it deep inside, in their heart. I challenged them to listen, to meditate very quietly, and I gave them the promise that if they would do this they would hear or feel this voice. Many sneered and jeered at this idea.

I responded to this ridicule by renewing the challenge: I asked each person to try it for himself, and if each person did not hear such a voice in one minute, the group could immediately dismiss me and I wouldn't waste any more of their time. This sobered them, and most appeared willing to experiment. I asked them to be very quiet and to do no talking, but to listen internally and ask themselves: "Is this chastity, as it has been explained this evening, a true principle or not?"

The first few seconds some looked around to see who was going to take this business seriously, but within about 20 seconds almost every person was sitting quietly and appeared to be very intent in thinking and listening. Many bowed their heads. After a full minute of silence, which probably seemed like an eternity to some, I looked at the individual at my left who had been so persuasive and vocal and said to him, "In all honesty, my friend, what did you hear?"

He responded, quietly but directly, "What I heard I did not say."

I turned to another who had been disagreeing and I asked him what he had heard.

He answered, "I do not know — I just don't know. I'm not certain any more."

One fellow stood up spontaneously in the rear. "I want to say something to my fraternity brothers I have never said before. I believe in God." Then he sat down.

Brother Covey talked about the same feeling my young friends and I felt in Primary — and he talked about the "powerful effects" Alma mentions. He said:

A totally different spirit came to that group, a spirit that had distilled gradually and silently during that minute of silence. I believe it was the spirit of the Lord or the spirit of Jesus Christ they felt inside. It had some interesting effects upon them. For one thing, they became subdued and quiet and rather reverent from then on. For another, it communicated worth to them. They became less intellectual and defensive and more open and teachable. I believe it also met a real need and confirmed some hopes and perhaps convicted others.

It was easy to teach them from then on. I felt as if seed was falling on fertile soil.[1]

THE BURDEN OF BOREDOM

So if the word of God is more powerful than a sword — as Brother Covey and, maybe, my Primary lesson, suggest — why is it possible to be bored at church?

An example: When my kids were young, every Sunday at dinner my wife and I would ask what they learned in Primary. Our older kids, Paul and Emily, typically shared details about their lessons, and our youngest, Melissa, shared a simpler report. One Sunday when Melissa was about three we asked how her Sunbeam class was. She started to say "fine," then stopped and said, "It was *boring.*"

I didn't buy it. Something was fishy. "Melissa," I asked, "what does 'boring' mean?"

She shrugged her shoulders. "Me don't know," she said. "That what Paul says."

Paul, who was eight, understood what boring is, and I think the rest of us understand it, too. You can see a lot of bishoprics understanding it every Sunday across the Church. I think it happens way too often. Look around next time you're in sacrament meeting or Sunday School; you'll see a lot of other people looking around, too.

So on the one hand we have the preaching of the word, which is more powerful than a sword — which can help us learn and understand the principles and lessons that can help us change our lives and live the way the Lord wants us to live. And on the other hand, we're either sleeping through it or we're fidgeting and not paying attention. Which leads to the fundamental question of this book: How can the talks and lessons we hear at church and gospel discussions in our homes change our lives if we're not listening?

Richard G. Scott, who served as an apostle for 27 years, shared the answer in an October 1993 conference talk. He said: "As you seek spiritual knowledge, seek for principles...Principles are concentrated truth, packaged for application in a wide variety of circumstances. *It is worth great effort to organize the truth we gather into simple statements of principle*" (italics added).[2]

To answer the question — How can the things we hear at church impact us if we're sleeping through them, or monkeying with our phones? — here are three simple statements of principle that will help you give a better talk, which David O. McKay shared in 1905:

1. Have an objective
2. Use examples
3. Emphasize application

THE POWER OF PRINCIPLES

Boyd K. Packer defined a gospel principle like this: "An enduring truth, a law, a rule you can adopt to guide you in making decisions."[3] In business and in health care, principles are sometimes called "best practices" — they're protocols that are proven to deliver the best possible outcomes.

"Generally principles are not spelled out in detail," Elder Packer said. "That leaves you free to find your way with an enduring truth, a principle, as your anchor." For example, the Church is founded on the principle of continuing revelation, which Elder Packer illustrated like this in a 1984 address to regional representatives:

In stake leadership meetings, I frequently ask a young elders quorum president about the procedure of calling a new counselor. *How would you call a new counselor?* The following is, I am very happy to report, typical of what happens.

The president says, "Well, first, I would go over the names of my quorum members in my mind and select the one who impresses me that he should be my counselor. Then I would pray about it."

"Why do you pray about it?"

"To receive direction from the Lord."

"What kind of direction?"

"To know whether it is right or not."

"You mean revelation?"

"Yes."

"You think you can receive revelation on such a thing?"

"Yes."

"Are you certain?"

"Yes."

"But you are a very ordinary young man; do you really believe you can get revelation from God?"

"Yes, sir!"

"Have you received it before?"

"Yes."

"I'm not going to be able to talk you out of it, am I?"

"No, sir!"

Just think of that! An ordinary young elders quorum president knows what revelation is and how to receive it. An ordinary young man knows how to approach the Lord through the veil and get revealed instruction...

That is a principle of the gospel. It is a law of God that he will reveal his will to his servants. Not just to the prophets and apostles, but to his servants across the world. It is a precious principle that must be guarded and nurtured.[4]

"Come, Follow Me" — the website and weekly scripture study manual that helps to make gospel learning home-centered and Church-supported — shares this advice as you teach the gospel in your home: *"Focus on principles that will bless your family. As you study the scriptures, ask yourself, 'What do I find here that will be especially meaningful to my family?'"*[5]

Some examples of principles in the scriptures: The grace of the Lord will help your weaknesses become strengths (Ether 12:27), give and it shall be given unto you (Luke 6:38), the Lord won't give you any commandments without preparing a way for you to fulfill them (1 Nephi 3:7), the Holy Ghost can help you can know the truth of all things (Moroni 10:5), and listen before you speak (James 1:19). Live your life by the principles in the scriptures, and you'll know the truth of what the Lord said in John 13:17: "If ye know these things, happy are ye if ye do them" (which is *another* great scriptural principle).

General conference, too, is packed with principles. Some that have jumped out at me over the years:

- When you do good, you feel good. (Ezra Taft Benson, April 1989)
- The Lord loves effort. (Russell M. Nelson, April 2020)
- Once we begin to see the divinity in ourselves, we can see it in others. (Rosemary M. Wixom, October 2015)
- The best paths in life are rarely the easiest. (Carlos A. Godoy, October 2014)
- Addictions are easier to prevent than to cure. (Dieter F. Uchtdorf, April 2014)
- Eternity is the wrong thing to be wrong about. (Joy D. Jones, April 2021)
- The Lord's hand in our lives is often clearest in hindsight. (Gerrit W. Gong, April 2016)
- When we choose to follow Jesus Christ, we choose to be changed. (Thierry K. Mutombo, April 2021)
- Doing things the Lord's way makes us happier than doing things our way. (J. Devn Cornish, October 2011)
- Faith takes work. (Russell M. Nelson, April 2021)

HOW A SCRIPTURAL PRINCIPLE DRAMATICALLY AFFECTED ME

Here's a personal example of a principle that had a dramatic impact on my life. In 1986, when I was 28, my wife and I had two young children, a frightening mortgage, and a leaky roof — and I'd just been laid off from my job. Two months into my job search, I was invited for an interview with a prominent company that had a job that seemed perfect for me. My first interview went very well; I made an immediate connection with the young manager who interviewed me and our visit was relaxed and comfortable; it felt more like a conversation than an interview. During our visit, the manager emphasized how the members of his department supported each other; teamwork was a high priority there, he said. I liked hearing that; the work environment and the job itself sounded ideal.

As the appointment was ending, the manager pointed to a tall stack of papers on the corner his desk. He said: *These are the resumes of the people who've applied for this job.* I blanched. He said: *We've had about 150 applicants.* The stack of resumes was a foot and a half high.

On the way home I was filled with joy — and despair. The job was exactly what I was looking for. The work looked engaging and fulfilling, the company was very successful, and the salary and benefits were good. But on the other hand, I thought: With 150 applicants for the job, my chances of getting it can be mathematically rounded off to zero — and unless I'm the top candidate, I'll end up in a 149-way tie for last place.

And then I thought about a scriptural principle I'd learned eight years earlier in the mission field. It's from Alma 29:4: *God grants unto men according to his desires.* Hartman Rector, Junior, my mission president, had emphasized that principle vigorously and repeatedly during my mission. There were nuances that affected its fulfillment, he said, but he repeated Alma's promise: What you really desire — not what you wish for, but what you *desire*, which means what you'll work and work and work for — you'll get.

So I got home from my interview and thought: *I'll partner up with Alma. I'll desire this job more than anyone else desires it.* I remembered the manager's emphasis on teamwork, and I had an idea: I'll show them — as opposed to tell them — I'm a team player, and I'll send a tangible metaphor that's so bulky the manager will have no choice but to put it on TOP of the stack of resumes on his desk. That will help me stand out.

I found my old Little League baseball mitt, put it in a box, and dropped in a note that summarized my experience as a team player and closed with this line: "I have the tools to join your team." I had the box delivered, and a week or two later I got a call to come in for a second interview. That time I met with the manager and his boss, and during our visit we talked about the department's team environment again, and I emphasized my teambuilding experience, as illustrated by my well-worn mitt. The interview went well.

Then: A speed bump. I learned there was an applicant who had an inside track for the job. She'd worked with some of the members of the staff before; they knew her and liked her. She was clearly the favored candidate for the position.

But she was competing against Alma and me. After my second interview I went to Deseret Industries and bought an old pair of scuffed-up baseball cleats. I cleaned them up and did my best to deodorize them, then put them in a shoe box with a note that recounted my experience. My message: "I have *lots* of mileage doing the work your team does."

Soon I was invited in for a third, and final, interview. Two finalists remained: The favored candidate — and me. This interview was with the department's five-member team. It started with a bang: The staff members gushed about my mitt and cleats — they talked about my creativity and teambuilding skills so much that I didn't have to. They clearly understood the skills I'd tried to emphasize, and our visit was fun, which is unusual in a job interview.

After that final visit, I knew Human Resources would be checking references, so I came up with one more baseball metaphor. I bought a can of chewing tobacco and dropped it off with a brief note that said: "I have no disgusting personal habits."

A day or two later the manager called and offered me the job. He said: *We really liked the other candidate, but she just couldn't stand up against the flood of clever stuff you kept sending in. You made our choice easy.*

I thought: Alma's promise made the difference; God *does* grant unto you according to your desires. Knowing that principle — and acting on it — made a huge difference in my career, and in my life.

THE SPECIFIC POWER OF PRESIDENT MCKAY'S THREE TEACHING PRINCIPLES

I included a promise at the beginning of this book: David O. McKay's three teaching principles can change your life — and the lives of everyone who listens to you speak or teach. They're very simple, and their simplicity enhances their power. If this book came with a money-back guarantee, it would be this: Your lessons and talks will dramatically improve if, every time you're asked to give a talk or teach a lesson and before every "Come, Follow Me" discussion in your home, you ask yourself:

1. What should my objective be?
2. What examples can I use to illustrate my objective?
3. How can I emphasize application?

President McKay shared those three principles a year before he was called as an apostle. He was 32. He'd been serving as a member of the Sunday School board of the Weber Stake near Ogden, Utah. He'd been home from his mission to Scotland for just five years and was working as the principal of the Weber Stake Academy (which later became Weber State University).

President McKay was tall, handsome, charismatic, funny, warm, and wise — and he was a powerful speaker. After his call to the Quorum of the Twelve in 1906, he was called in 1934 to the First Presidency and called as prophet in 1951, and served in that role for 19 years. A number of historians say his influence helped facilitate the growth of the early, Utah-centric church into a worldwide religion.

And his skill as a teacher was legendary. BYU's School of Education is named after him, and Weber State's College of Education is housed in the McKay Education Building. One historian listed a number of the things he excelled at — academics, athletics, music, public speaking, and leadership — then said his greatest talent was teaching.[6] After President McKay died in 1970, Joseph Fielding Smith — who succeeded him as Prophet — said: "For all time to come men shall rise up and call his name blessed."[7] My sense is: As you consider and apply his advice on how to speak or teach, you'll call his name blessed, too.

Valoy Eaton was a young boy living in eastern Utah when President McKay came to his stake as a member of the First Presidency to dedicate a new chapel. Brother Eaton, who grew up to become a noted painter, remembers:

When I saw President McKay I had the same impression some other people have had, as I witnessed a spiritual glow which radiated from him, but this sort of thing was a new experience for me. After the meeting, even though I was somewhat intimidated, my mother placed me in line with some other children to shake his hand. This was almost 60 years ago but I still remember vividly the indescribable feeling which came into my being when he shook my hand and said a few cheerful words to me.[8]

A brief example of President McKay's skill as a speaker: In April 1956, in a general conference address titled "Harmony in the Home," he listed three virtues that strengthen marriage. One of them — self-control — built on a comment he'd made earlier: "Let husband and wife never speak to one another in loud tones, unless the house is on fire." In conference he said:

Little things happen that annoy you, and you speak quickly, sharply, loudly, and wound the other's heart. I know of no virtue that helps to contribute to the happiness and peace of the home more than that great quality of self-control in speech. Refrain from saying the sharp word that comes to your mind at once if you are wounded or if you see something in the other which offends you. It is said that during courtship we should keep our eyes wide open, but after marriage keep them half-shut.

What I mean may be illustrated by a young woman who said to her husband, "I know that my cooking isn't good; I hate it as much as you do, but do you find me sitting around griping about it?" Griping after marriage is what makes it unpleasant. I recall the words of Will Carleton:

> Boys flying kites haul in their white-winged birds —
> You can't do that when you're flying words.
> Thoughts unexpressed may sometimes fall back dead
> But God himself can't kill them when they're said. [9]

President McKay's power as a speaker was so influential that a book on his speeches and speaking style — titled *The Rhetoric of David O. McKay* — was published in 1993 as part of a national academic series on religion and theology. "His charisma and legend began an upward spiral among fellow members of the LDS Church...and this intramural admiration eventually affected many non-Mormon opinion leaders as well," says the book. "The LDS Church experienced its greatest prosperity, to that point, under McKay's direction. It has been the contention here that prosperity finally visited a heretofore very unpopular and out-of-the-way organization due, certainly in part, to David O. McKay...It can be argued that McKay's success may also be attributed to what some would argue is the most effective of all rhetorical phenomena, which Quintilian simply enunciated as 'a good man skilled in speaking.'" [10]

Harold B. Lee described his influence more succinctly. "The world produces few David McKays," he said, "and it's those few who change the world." [11]

BUT WHAT IF YOU DON'T LIKE SPEAKING IN CHURCH?

If you're not a world-changing leader — or charismatic or poetic or funny or even wise — can you still say something people will remember in 60 years? Or in 60 minutes?

Yes. You can — and you should. In Doctrine and Covenants 88:77, the Lord says, "And I give unto you a commandment that you shall teach one another the doctrine of the kingdom." President McKay's three principles will help you fill that commandment *effectively*.

But before we address those principles, let me share three introductory points. First, the most important thing you can do to teach effectively in the Church and at home — in fact, the only thing that really matters — is to speak with the Spirit. A number of powerful conference talks reiterate that theme, and a terrific book titled *Teaching By The Spirit* by Elder Gene R. Cook, an emeritus member of the First Quorum of the Seventy, addresses the topic in specific detail. It's powerful and inspiring, and it has a different focus than this book. Elder Cook's book will enhance your ability to teach with the Spirit. This book will help you speak effectively, so people will listen to you, and so when the Spirit speaks through you, they'll be paying attention.

It's hard to influence anyone who's not listening. To use the wonderful metaphor Alma uses,[12] the Spirit is the seed that will sprout in the hearts of the people who are touched by the things you say. President McKay's three principles give you a shovel, a hose, and some Miracle-Gro.

Second, a word about my background. What qualifies me to tell you about the three principles that will help you teach effectively? The answer is, I've practiced them for almost 40 years in a wide range of speaking and teaching roles. I used them professionally when I was a speechwriter for a number of political and business leaders (starting back when speeches were *speeches*, not PowerPoint presentations). I've practiced them at church as a missionary, a gospel doctrine teacher, a bishop, and in other callings. I've used them in my work, where I've presented to numerous professional and public audiences (and accepted invitations to serve as a paid lecturer on topics ranging from health care reform to humor in the workplace).

I first heard President McKay's three speaking principles when I was serving a mission in early 1977. They struck me so forcefully I wrote them in the notes section of my Bible. I don't remember who shared them or how they were presented, but I recognized they were worth remembering, and as I started to use them, I saw: They really work. Later in my mission I served in our mission office when Elder Hartman Rector, Junior, of the First Quorum of the Seventy was our mission president. In that role I gave the same talk 10 different times in the zone conferences of our mission's 10 zones, month after month for seven months. By the time we finished each round of conferences, my companion could give my talk verbatim and I could give his. That's when I learned to speak in public. All that repetitive practice showed me that President McKay's three principles helped me connect with the people I was speaking to and convey the messages I felt the Lord wanted me to share.

I kept using the three principles when I got home. The sacrament meeting talk I gave to report my mission on June 11, 1978, turned out to be the most important talk I've ever given — because my future wife, Laurie Evans, was there in the meeting, and she was there with her *boyfriend*. I wrote in my journal that the talk felt like another zone conference; the Spirit joined me as I spoke and I felt like I connected with the congregation. I had an objective (testify that the Church is true and that the Lord speaks to us as we follow Him), used examples (I had two years' worth of stories, some of them funny), and emphasized application (talk with our friends and neighbors about the gospel; share our testimonies in word and deed). One of my stories: Shortly before my mission ended, I remembered talking to a recently returned missionary who'd come home to the ward where I was serving. He was reporting his mission that day and he was nervous about his talk. I shook his hand and said I was glad it was him speaking and not me. He asked how long I had left and I said about a month, and he quoted Mosiah 17:18, which says: "Ye shall suffer, as I suffer."

After my talk, Laurie told me later that she turned to her boyfriend and said: "*That's* my idea of what a returned missionary is like." She meant that in a good way, and about two years later, once we started dating, when I tried to convince her I had potential, the field was white, already to harvest.

Which leads to my final point of introduction. You'll recognize the effectiveness of President McKay's principles by their fruits. What I say about his seven powerful words of counsel won't mean as much as what you'll see when you practice them. You'll see they're *concentrated truth*, to use Elder Scott's words.

Use them next time you give a talk or teach a lesson. Watch what happens. In *Jesus The Christ,* James E. Talmage emphasizes a powerful phrase that's repeated several times in the New Testament, first by Jesus and then by Phillip: *Come and see.* Elder Talmage writes: "The man who would know Christ must come to Him, to see and hear, to feel and know... Are you in doubt as to what that message means today? Then come and see for yourself. Would you know where Christ is to be found? Come and see." [13]

So come and see. Test the three principles President McKay shared and see if they help you.

One addendum: Given the importance of teaching the gospel in the home — as supported by the focus on home-centered, Church-supported gospel learning — President McKay's three principles have never been more timely. They express what you probably already know intuitively: Objective-oriented stories that encourage us to apply the lessons they contain have been shared among families and friends well before there were Family Home Evenings or "Come, Follow Me" manuals.

A story my mom shared when I was very young wasn't part of a lesson or a home evening. Her parents were farmers in a small Nevada town, and when they retired and sold their farm, they moved to a big city, where my grandpa encountered something he'd never seen before — traffic lights. One day, as grandpa drove through an intersection, the light above him turned red, which horrified him. He drove around the block, approached the same intersection again, turned off to the side of the road and waited for the light to turn red, then pulled back into the street and waited until the light turned green so he could demonstrate his commitment to obey the law.

Grandpa died when I was only 1, but I've always remembered that story. And the principle I learned was, I have a legacy to uphold of doing what's right and correcting the mistakes I make along the way.

CLARIFYING QUESTIONS: THE POWER OF PRINCIPLES

Share your answers and see what others have posted at BetterTalksLDS.com.

1. What's one principle that has shaped your life?

2. What principles did you learn when you were young?

3. How did you learn the principles that have influenced you — did you learn them on your own or did someone teach them to you?

4. What gospel principles are most important to you?

5. When has applying a principle made a difference in your life — in your relationships, at church, or at work?

HAVE AN OBJECTIVE

Here's an example of how an objective increases the power and effectiveness of a talk. In 1999, John Butler, a convert to the Church from California, stood up and stated his objective like this at the start of a sacrament meeting talk he delivered on Valentine's Day — Sunday, February 14: *"Here's how I know the Lord loves me."*

He said he prays every day for the Lord to *watch over and protect* his family, using that specific phrase. He said he's used it so much it became almost rote, then he said: Let me tell you how I've seen the Lord answer that prayer.

John told this story. He and his wife, Maren, and their young family spent a week on a houseboat at Lake Powell one summer. They prayed at night, like they usually do; John remembers asking the Lord to watch over and protect his family, just like usual, then everyone climbed into their sleeping bags and went to sleep. But in the middle of the night, one of their sons — who was two — got up, walked along the houseboat's outer walkway, and decided to see if he could climb into the speedboat that was bumping against their houseboat's bumper. The boy had loved riding in the speedboat during their week at the lake, and getting in it again looked enticing.

So he leaned over, his feet on the houseboat, his hands on the speedboat, and tried to climb into the speedboat, but it started to drift away. He stretched out over the water as a gap appeared between the two boats, first a foot, then two feet —

And as the two boats drifted apart, something woke John up. He sat up. He knew something was wrong. He got up quickly and walked to the deck, where he saw his young son, stretched out between the two boats, and grabbed him before he dropped into the water. "He fell the moment I reached down to grab him," John said.

The boy was safe. John said in our sacrament meeting: "One reason I know the Lord loves me is because he answers my prayers, like he answered that prayer."[14]

I was in the meeting when John spoke, and here's one way to measure the power of his words: Ever since then, every morning, I've prayed for the Lord to watch over and protect *my* family.

WHY A GOOD OBJECTIVE MAKES A DIFFERENCE

It's easy to tell the objective of a lot of talks and lessons at church: Use up the time! The second most popular objective (which is often used in concert with the first): Cover the topic! (Or, in a lesson, cover the material in the manual.)

But remember this advice next time you prepare a talk or a lesson: *Feed my sheep.*

President Dallin H. Oaks said this in an October 1999 conference talk: "A gospel teacher, like the Master we serve, will concentrate entirely on those being taught. His or her total concentration will be on the needs of the sheep — the good of the students. A gospel teacher does not focus on himself or herself. One who understands that principle will not look upon his or her calling as 'giving or presenting a lesson,' because that definition views teaching from the standpoint of the teacher, not the student."

Or, in other words, if your focus is on covering the material or using up the time, it's time to rethink your objective.

Elder Whitney L. Clayton of the Seventy reiterated President Oaks' point in a talk titled "Teach People, Not Lessons." He talked about a very knowledgeable family history consultant who was an especially skilled teacher (and who knew way more about family history than Elder Clayton did). He said: "I have thought that what he did with me was just what missionaries are taught to do in *Preach My Gospel.* He understood that he wasn't teaching lessons; he was teaching me. It would probably have been easier for him to simply start at page one of the lessons and take me through the material without thinking much about what I knew or didn't know, and without worrying much about what I had understood or was remembering. But he was teaching me, not the lessons, so he focused on me and on my needs and interests."[15]

President Thomas S. Monson, in an article titled "How to Communicate Effectively," said: "One must make his presentation clear. The first rule of clarity is to have a well-defined goal or objective — to know what you wish to accomplish through your communication. *Unless you can define this goal clearly to yourself, it is not likely your audience will understand it and be motivated* (italics added)."[16]

Brigham Young heard some talks where the objective was murky. He said: "It is a great fault in the elders of Israel, when they talk to a congregation, that they speak a great while about something, but you cannot always easily tell what."[17]

The solution, President McKay said, is to *have an objective.*

MAKE YOUR FIRST FEW WORDS COUNT

It's tempting when you start a talk to begin with something funny or to relate how you got the assignment to speak — a joke can connect you with the congregation and that kind of opening helps you feel comfortable. But the key word there is *you*, and remember: *You* are not your focus. Don't give in to that temptation.

Here's a secret: Having (and expressing) a specific, inspired objective is more engaging — and more entertaining — than being entertaining. If you have something to say, and you start saying it, you'll be more interesting, and you'll feel more comfortable, than if you wander into your talk. "You've got to center on one idea, one theme, and give it in the first sentence or paragraph," said Elder Boyd K. Packer. "Then let everything from there on support it. Let your audience know right up front what you're talking about and don't keep them guessing."[18]

Keep King Benjamin's address in mind. When he gathered his people to hear the final words he'd share as their prophet, he was very clear about what he had to say as he began his talk: "I have not commanded you to come up hither to trifle with the words which I shall speak."[19] In other words: "I'm not here to waste your time. I'm here to deliver the message and fulfill the objective God gave me to fill." You hear a statement like that and you sit up straight and take notes. That's the power a strong objective gives you, especially when you introduce it directly and plainly.

In a one-hour sacrament meeting, being concise will benefit you, whoever else speaks, and everyone who's listening. But it's hard; the nervousness you'll feel when you stand up makes it awkward to jump into your talk without some kind of preamble. Mark Twain described that aspect of human nature when he said, "I didn't have time to write a short letter, so I wrote a long one instead." But the less you wander, the faster you'll get where you're going.

Here are examples of the first few sentences in the talks delivered in just one weekend of general conference — April 2013. I chose that conference completely at random to see the opening lines of the talks. Here's what I found:

- Elder David A. Bednar: "My message addresses a fundamental question of great spiritual consequence: Why is the law of chastity so important?"

- Elder Quentin R. Cook: "Recent experiences have caused me to reflect on the doctrine of peace and especially the role of Jesus Christ in helping each of us obtain lasting personal peace."

- Elder Enrique R. Falabella: "Some parents excuse themselves for mistakes they have made at home, stating that the reason for this is that there is not a school for parenting. In reality, such a school does exist and it can be the best of all. This school is called home."

- Sister Elaine S. Dalton, Young Women general president: "Every week young women all over the world repeat the Young Women theme. No matter the language, each time I hear these words, 'We are daughters of our Heavenly Father, who loves us, and we love Him,' the Spirit affirms to my soul that they are true. It is not only an affirmation of our identity — who we are — but also an acknowledgment of *Whose* we are. We are daughters of an exalted being!"

- Elder Richard G. Scott: "Many voices from the world in which we live tell us we should live at a frantic pace. There is always more to do and more to accomplish. Yet deep inside each of us is a need to have a place of refuge where peace and serenity prevail, a place where we can reset, regroup, and reenergize to prepare for future pressures. The ideal place for that peace is within the walls of our own homes, where we have done all we can to make the Lord Jesus Christ the centerpiece."

Speaking of powerful and concise objectives shared in general conference, it would almost be a sin to not include the introduction of Elder

Bruce R. McConkie's talk in April 1985, which was his last address as an apostle, delivered two weeks before he died of cancer. He stood up and stated the objective of his talk with one sentence:

> I feel, and the Spirit seems to accord, that the most important doctrine I can declare, and the most powerful testimony I can bear, is one of the atoning sacrifice of the Lord Jesus Christ.

That's *exactly* how to state your objective when you give a talk. Anyone who's ever hemmed and hawed when you stand up to speak, anyone who's begun a talk by recounting how you were asked to speak, and anyone who's tempted to begin with a joke or feels a need to say you didn't quite do all the preparation you meant to do — all of us can be enlightened by Elder McConkie's example.[20]

He told us plainly and simply what he was going to talk about. He used 35 words, arranged in one sentence, and none of the words had more than three syllables. His testimony was woven into those words, and they were injected with so much spiritual and personal power that members of the Church around the world today — over three decades later — remember his voice, his words, and his testimony. It's the best example of a well-stated objective I can think of.

A PERSONAL AND HISTORIC EXAMPLE
OF THE IMPACT OF AN OBJECTIVE

The "Come, Follow Me" manual that outlined a year of New Testament study taught my wife and me a powerful lesson during the week we discussed the Savior's crucifixion. The manual recounted the Lord's compassion for his mother and the mercy he expressed to his crucifiers "even during His own incomparable suffering." The text said, "In His final moments on earth, Jesus was doing what He had done throughout his mortal ministry — teaching us by showing us."[21] When Laurie and I read those words, we paused to discuss what they meant: The Lord was true to his covenants and he was consistent in his behavior — he was kind, patient, and forgiving — even while he was being crucified.

Or, in terms that were relative to us: He kept his commitments even when he wasn't feeling well. That theme became the objective of our "Come, Follow Me" discussion that week; in fact, that was one of the major themes we took away from our year of study. As my wife and I get older, often we don't feel well. We're tired. We both have health issues. But we can still keep our covenants and do our duty no matter how we feel — because we saw what the Lord did when he was suffering.

That principle is underscored by a story told by Jeffrey R. Holland: "A student once told Harvard dean LeBaron Russell Briggs that he hadn't done his assignment because he hadn't felt well. Looking the student piercingly in the eye, Dean Briggs said, 'Mr. Smith, I think in time you may perhaps find that most of the work in the world is done by people who aren't feeling very well.'"[22]

Here's another unforgettable objective from a different kind of speech you may recognize, which begins like this: "Four score and seven years ago our fathers brought forth on this continent a new nation, conceived in liberty, and dedicated to the proposition that all men are created equal." Abraham Lincoln, speaking at Gettysburg, Pennsylvania, on November 19, 1863, went on to say:

> Now we are engaged in a great civil war, testing whether that nation, or any nation so conceived and so dedicated, can long endure. We are met on a great battlefield of that war. We have come to dedicate a portion of that field, as a final resting place for those who here gave their lives that that nation might live. It is altogether fitting and proper that we should do this.
>
> But, in a larger sense, we cannot dedicate, we cannot consecrate, we cannot hallow this ground. The brave men, living and dead, who

struggled here have consecrated it far above our poor power to add or detract. The world will little note nor long remember what we say here, but it can never forget what they did here. It is for us, the living, rather, to be dedicated here to the unfinished work which they who fought here have thus far so nobly advanced. It is rather for us to be here dedicated to the great task remaining before us — that from these honored dead we take increased devotion to that cause for which they gave the last full measure of devotion — that we here highly resolve that these dead shall not have died in vain — that this nation, under God, shall have a new birth of freedom — and that government of the people, by the people, for the people, shall not perish from the earth.

The Gettysburg Address doesn't have a formal introduction. President Lincoln doesn't say, "Gosh, I hardly had any time to prepare my talk today — I had to finish it on the back of an envelope on the way here! And boy, was the wagon bumpy as I wrote!" He doesn't say, "Before I begin, you know, a Catholic priest, a Latter-day Saint pioneer, and a blacksmith were in a covered wagon one day, and..." Instead the speech focuses immediately on what Lincoln was there to say. His objective — the most fitting way to remember those who are buried in this cemetery is to advance the cause they died for — is wrapped into every word of the speech. None of its 10 sentences are frivolous or wasted. No wonder everyone who went to elementary school in the United States remembers it.

HOW YOUR *OBJECTIVE* MAY BE DIFFERENT THAN YOUR *TOPIC*

When you pray and ponder about what your objective should be, it's easy to revert to a default objective — which is the topic you've been assigned. Isn't it, as President Lincoln might say, altogether fitting and proper to do that? The answer is, sometimes you'll be asked to address a topic that clearly outlines your objective. But sometimes your topic and your objective will be different; your topic will be assigned, but your objective is up to you. If your topic is *faith*, for example, your objective might be to *help the members of the ward increase their faith by studying the scriptures every day.* If your text is the Book of Enos in the Book of Mormon, your objective might be: *Praying with real intent and keeping records can help you grow spiritually.*

Your objective is the message you want your listeners to take away from your talk; your goal is to plant that message deep in their hearts. Ezra Taft Benson described what I'm talking about: "When we set goals, we are in command," he said. "If we can state our goals clearly, we will gain a purpose and meaning in all our actions. Clearly understood goals bring our lives into focus just as a magnifying glass focuses a beam of light into a burning point. Without goals our efforts may be scattered and unproductive."[23]

I love the story Joseph Fielding McConkie — the son of Elder Bruce R. McConkie of the Quorum of the Twelve — told about topic-related advice his dad gave him when he returned from a tour of duty as a military chaplain:

> After my return from military service in Vietnam, I received a number of invitations to speak at firesides. Concerned that I was being invited to entertain with faith-promoting stories rather than to teach gospel principles, and, moreover, that those stories might appreciably improve with continued telling, I asked Dad what I should do. His counsel was to accept the invitations to speak and then "have the good sense to speak on what they should have asked you to speak on in the first place."[24]

Again, let me emphasize: I'm *not* suggesting you choose the topic you address. That's been assigned, either by your bishopric or in the manual you're using as a gospel teacher. But I am saying: *Use the topic you've been given and mold it into an objective based on guidance from the Spirit and your understanding of the needs of the people you'll address.*

President McKay said: "The aim (or objective) is the general truth the lesson proves or illustrates." He used this analogy: "The aim is the immaterial something that strikes the soul, as the aroma of the orange does the sense of smell." [25]

FIVE STEPS TO HELP YOU DETERMINE YOUR OBJECTIVE

So how can you form your objective? Follow these five steps:

1. BE SPECIFIC. That's so important I need to repeat it for emphasis. Be specific. Be specific. Be specific. If your bishop has asked you to talk about faith, for example, choose a specific component of faith you can focus on — such as: Faith is a principle of action that's helped me in my mission, my career, and in finding the person I married. I think when a speaker stands up and shares an objective like that, you automatically perk up: *Faith helped you in your mission* and *your career? And it helped you find your spouse?* Right there, they want to know what happened. They're paying attention.

2. BE ACTION-ORIENTED (see more on that in chapter four). President McKay said: "It is not enough to know what is good, we must do good." Keep that in mind.[26]

3. FOCUS ON THE NEEDS OF THE PEOPLE YOU'RE SPEAKING TO. We've talked about that already, but Elder Gene R. Cook of the Seventy focused specifically on considering their needs *before you prepare* your talk or lesson — or in other words, as you're choosing your objective. He said: "Each time you are preparing to speak, truly ponder beforehand what the needs of the people might be."[27]

4. RELY ON THE SPIRIT. Brigham Young said: "Anything besides that influence will fail to convince any person of the truth of the gospel of salvation."[28] I've found: The Spirit will lead you not only in what you say, but in what your objective should be.

5. PAY ATTENTION TO THE STATEMENTS IN CHURCH LESSON MANUALS THAT IDENTIFY THE PURPOSE OF EACH LESSON. If you're a teacher, the manuals give you a terrific head start in choosing an objective by listing the purpose of the lesson right below the lesson title. But I worry that line is too often ignored. For example, a lot of teachers introduce their lesson by saying: *Today we're going to talk about the Good Samaritan* — without considering the purpose the gospel doctrine teacher's manual includes, which is: *To help class members humble themselves, forgive others, and show charity for one another.* When you say you're going to talk about the Good Samaritan, you're talking about your text. When you say you'll be talking about helping your class be humble, forgive, and show charity, you're talking about *your class members.*

A SPECIFIC EXAMPLE OF
THE IMPORTANCE OF BEING SPECIFIC

Let me be more specific about the first point I mentioned — be specific. If you're reading a paper copy of this book, underline this line: *The more specific your objective is, the more effective your talk or lesson will be.*

Here's an example. Years ago when I was teaching gospel doctrine, I opened the manual a few days before Sunday and saw the topic was the Sabbath day. I thought: *Oh, great. I've taught a bunch of lessons on the Sabbath, and our people in the class have discussed it a thousand times. What more can we say? How can I make this interesting?*

That interior monologue, by the way, was in the form of a whine. But then I got a little more serious. I thought: *No, really, how can I make a lesson on the Sabbath day spiritually compelling? How can our discussion help the members of our class grow spiritually and learn how to keep the Sabbath more effectively?* Those kinds of questions started to stir in my mind and heart. I stopped whining and started thinking. I grew humble; I prayed for help. And then this idea crossed my mind: *I could ask the class to focus on one thing that could help them improve the way they keep the Sabbath.* I thought: *What's the thing?* The answer, with spiritual clarity, was: *I don't know — that's for each member of the class to decide.*

So on Sunday when I stood up to start the lesson, I talked about a part in the movie "City Slickers" where an old cowboy, played by Jack Palance, tells a customer at a dude ranch, played by Billy Crystal: The secret to life is just one thing. Billy's character says: Yeah, so? What's the one thing? And Jack Palance says: That's what you've got to figure out.

I told the class: D&C 59:14 says the Sabbath should be a day of rejoicing, and Isaiah says we should call the Sabbath a delight — but do we rejoice? And is it delightful? I said: The point of today's lesson is: There's one thing that can help us increase the blessings of the Sabbath — possibly dramatically. I don't know what it is, but I'll pass out notepaper so you can write it down when you sense it.

We spent the next 20 minutes discussing points from the manual — which, truly, everyone had heard before — about keeping the Sabbath day. They ranged from understanding why the Lord commanded us to honor the Sabbath to partaking mindfully of the sacrament to resting from our labors to doing good on the Sabbath. After our discussion, with 15 or 20 minutes of class time left, I asked people to write down one thing that would help them make Sunday more meaningful, then we discussed their ideas. I remember our discussion was gripping and spiritually engaging, and I remember walking out of Sunday School thinking of one thing I could do: Focus more on the words of the hymns we sing. I'm a horrible singer, and my main goal during the hymns is to sing softly enough so I don't drive whoever I'm sitting by out of the chapel screaming, but I thought: I can pay more attention to those sacred words, and focus on their meaning, even if I can't sing them well.

The lesson reminded me of what Marion G. Romney said: "I always know when I am speaking under the influence of the Holy Ghost because I always learn something from what I have said."[29] That's exactly the way I felt when our lesson ended.

SOME SAMPLE TOPICS AND OBJECTIVES

Let's try this: Here's a list of potential topics — along with good, and better, objectives. (I won't list the best objective because I can't; that's up to you, your insights into the needs of the people you're addressing, and the Spirit.) I hope it helps you choose an objective that will help you give a talk that has *a more powerful effect upon the minds of the people than the sword, or anything else, which had happened unto them.*

TOPIC: The scriptures
GOOD OBJECTIVE: The blessings of reading the scriptures regularly
BETTER OBJECTIVE: How I learned to read a chapter a day in the scriptures — and how that helps me see how the Lord answers my prayers

TOPIC: Ministering
GOOD OBJECTIVE: Two ways ministering has strengthened me spiritually
BETTER OBJECTIVE: How ministering has blessed me (and the people I shepherd) spiritually and practically

TOPIC: How to get a testimony
GOOD OBJECTIVE: How I received a testimony and how it's enhanced my life
BETTER OBJECTIVE: Three principles I learned in general conference about how we can get and maintain a testimony

TOPIC: Mother's Day
GOOD OBJECTIVE: Three ways my mother blessed my life
BETTER OBJECTIVE: Three ways my mother helped me learn to follow the Lord

TOPIC: Christmas
GOOD OBJECTIVE: The real spirit of Christmas
BETTER OBJECTIVE: Two Christmas gifts I received that weren't under the tree

TOPIC: The Sermon on the Mount
GOOD OBJECTIVE: How we can apply the Beatitudes in our lives
BETTER OBJECTIVE: How Matthew's account of the Sermon on the Mount differs from Luke's account — and what Orson Pratt said about those differences in volume 16 of the Journal of Discourses in 1873, as opposed to what George Q. Cannon said in volume 8 in 1861
NOTE: *Just kidding!*

AN EXAMPLE OF HOW TO STATE YOUR OBJECTIVE

Once you've set your objective, state it directly — and don't be shy about repeating it. Remember this advice from Boyd K. Packer: "Tell your listeners what you are going to tell them, tell them, and then tell them what you have told them."[30] That reiterates a marketing mantra I've heard many times: Repetition builds retention.

Elder Packer followed his own advice. I remember a powerful talk he gave in conference in October 1973 titled "Inspiring Music, Worthy Thoughts." He began his talk like this:

President (Harold B.) Lee concluded our last conference in April with the statement that in his 32 years as a General Authority he had learned that the most inspired preaching is always accompanied by beautiful, inspired music. I am grateful this morning to be sustained by the beautiful renditions of the choir.

"Music," Addison said, "is the only sensual gratification in which mankind may indulge to excess without injury to their moral or religious feelings."

If that were true in his day, it is not in ours. Music, once that innocent, now is often used for wicked purposes.

I was 16 when he gave that talk. I was only a casual conference watcher back then — but President Packer was talking to *me*, and he was talking about something I *loved.* To me at that time, there were only two kinds of music: Rock — and roll. I had a stereo in my room, purchased several years earlier with money I'd earned from a paper route, and I had a growing collection of albums, most of them by bands such as the Beatles, the Byrds, Chicago, the Moody Blues, etc. I loved that music.

But when Elder Packer stood at the podium in conference in October 1973, he told me what he was going to tell me. He said:

I would recommend that you go through your record albums and set aside those records that promote the so-called new morality, the drug or the hard rock culture. Such music ought not to belong to young people concerned about spiritual development.

Then he told me what he was telling me:

Why not go through your collection? Get rid of the worst of it. Keep just the best of it. Be selective in what you consume and what you produce. It becomes a part of you.

Then he told me what he'd told me:

Young people, you cannot afford to fill your mind with the unworthy hard music of our day. It is not harmless. It can welcome onto the stage of your mind unworthy thoughts and set the tempo to which they dance and to which you may act.[31]

That hit me with great force — enough that I decided to follow his advice. I went through my record collection and found a couple of albums I didn't think I should keep. I threw some away. Another album had a bunch of terrific songs I really liked — marred by one selection that was clearly offensive. I couldn't bear to get rid of the entire album, so I took a knife and scratched a deep cut through the vinyl grooves of the disagreeable song, which made the song unplayable. I also remember forbidding my brother, who didn't have a stereo in his room, from playing any of his inappropriate albums on my stereo. That annoyed him, and when I was 16, bugging my brother was an extra blessing that flowed from following Elder Packer's advice. Win/win!

YOUR OBJECTIVE IS THE KEY TRUTH YOU WANT TO SHARE

David O. McKay shared this advice about developing your objective when he chaired a church-wide Sunday School convention in 1907: "It [your objective] will be a unifying means, unifying the lesson, so that it may sink into the souls of the children."

He defined an objective (which he originally referred to as an "aim") like this: "The aim is the general truth that the lesson proves or illustrates…In the preparation of a lesson, an aim is an end; the lesson a means." He advised teachers to focus on their objective and take out elements that complicate it. "In the development of an aim, it is as necessary to study what *not* [my emphasis] to put into your lesson as to know what to introduce into it," he said. "That teacher is the most successful who eliminates all non-essentials."

And he added: "The aim is selected by a careful preview of the lesson and by contemplation and thought, with both lessons and pupils in mind. It is developed by using only the necessary points in the lesson, and what is as important, by grouping these points in a logical manner. The aim is applied by leading the pupils into avenues of action."[32]

A forceful example of each of those points — focus on the key truth you want to impart, take out nonessential materials, and organize your talk or lesson so it supports your objective — is found in a devotional address Elder Vai Sikahema delivered at BYU-Hawaii in January 2020. It's titled "Our Religious Obligation to be Educated."

Elder Sikahema was called to the Quorum of the Seventy in April 2021; he was an Area Seventy when the talk was given. He's a former BYU football player who played in the NFL for eight years, then worked as sports director for Philadelphia's NBC affiliate for twenty-six years. After a brief introduction, he stated his objective very clearly:

> This morning, I want to talk to you about our obligation to seek knowledge and an education.

He quoted President Russell M. Nelson, who said pursuing an education is a religious duty. Then he recounted his educational journey, which included a poverty-stricken childhood in Tonga, then a move to Arizona, where Elder Sikahema was a high school football star — but not a very good student. He described the college football coaches who poured into his home to recruit him. Then he said:

> We now faced a new challenge: qualifying me academically for those scholarship offers. My parents both worked long hours: mom as a factory seamstress and dad as a security guard. My parents were oblivious to my academic challenges. They never attended parent/teacher night because I didn't bother telling them. Why would I? I was making C's and D's.
>
> My mother had a visiting teacher named Barbara Nielsen. Sister Nielsen happened to be an English teacher at my high school and she was also the faculty advisor of the school newspaper. As I was excelling on the field, I was failing in the classroom. Sister Nielsen knew that. So she came to our home and told my mother, "Ruby, I

want Vai in my English class. And I want him to apply for a reporter position on the school newspaper. It will help him with his grammar and I'll teach him how to write. Unless he gets high marks on his SAT, I'm afraid he won't qualify to any of those prestigious schools recruiting him."

So, Barbara Nielsen came weekly — not monthly, but weekly. Together we read Dickens' *Great Expectations, Oliver Twist,* and *A Tale of Two Cities.* We read Harper Lee's *To Kill A Mockingbird* and Twain's *Adventures of Tom Sawyer* and *Huckleberry Finn.* We also did a deep dive into Harriett Beecher Stowe's *Uncle Tom's Cabin.* We didn't just read these classics, Sister Nielsen wanted to have "conversations" about them. She expected me to follow and understand the plot, be familiar with the central characters, the protagonists and antagonists. She wanted to know my opinion on why the authors cast Pip, Scout and Uncle Tom as the protagonist in their stories. *I don't know! I'm 16 years old!* I didn't say it, I just thought it. I could not believe my dumb luck! My English teacher is my mother's visiting teacher! I was a high school football star, but when Barbara Nielsen visited our home, my mother insisted that I sit at her side like a five-year-old. In a word, it was humiliating. You think my mother cared? Not ONE bit.

Today, Barbara Nielsen is in her 80s. I visited her a few years ago. She is the reason I qualified for BYU. She is the reason I graduated with a degree in broadcast journalism. Barbara Nielsen is the reason I'm anchoring television news in Philadelphia, the fourth largest TV market in the country. She is why within a generation of my parents' immigration from Tonga, we have reaped the rewards of an American education.

Because my angel mother didn't know how to navigate the American college system, she prayed and the Lord sent her Barbara Nielsen. What are the chances that my huge public high school's best English teacher and faculty advisor of the school newspaper would be in my ward? I believe Ruby Sikahema's prayers made it so.

Elder Sikahema went on to describe his family's educational achievements: His sister was then finishing her PhD; his brother had a degree in finance and a master's from BYU — and each one of the next generation of the Sikahema family had either graduated from college or were in the process.

Then Elder Sikahema reiterated his objective with another quote from President Nelson — he told us what he was telling us, as Elder Packer might say. He said:

> I close with this counsel from Pres. Nelson: "Because of our sacred regard for each human intellect, we consider the obtaining of an education to be a religious responsibility. Yet opportunities and abilities differ. I believe that in the pursuit of education, individual desire is more influential than institution, and personal faith more forceful than faculty...Our Creator expects His children everywhere to educate themselves. He issued a commandment: "Seek ye diligently and teach one another words of wisdom; yea, seek ye out of the best books words of wisdom; seek learning, even by study and also by faith." And He assures us that knowledge acquired here will be ours forever.

And finally, Elder Sikahema told us what he told us. He concluded his talk like this:

> My dear young friends, I pray for your success. That with your degree in hand, you will go build the Kingdom, whether here or abroad. Remembering always the BYU motto: Enter to Learn; Go Forth to Serve.[33]

When I heard that talk, my thought was: If Elder Sikahema played football like he speaks, no wonder he was All-Pro in the NFL!

ADVICE FOR TEACHERS (AS OPPOSED TO SPEAKERS): AN INSPIRED OBJECTIVE CAN HELP YOU ASK BETTER QUESTIONS

Here's a huge — HUGE — benefit of a good objective when you're teaching a lesson: It will help you ask better questions. That will enhance the discussion you have in your class, which is how the members of your class really learn. For example, if your objective as a gospel doctrine teacher is based on the text you're assigned to cover, as opposed to the needs of the class, your goal for a lesson on D&C 94-97 might be: Talk about building the Kirtland Temple. You'll probably start by asking a question like this: Well, our lesson today is on building the Kirtland Temple, so what do you know about how the temple was built?

And the response will be: Everyone in the room will avoid eye contact with you, which will be bad, and then a historian/gospel scholar in the class will recount some facts about how the temple was built, which will be worse. Right out of the chute, you're not teaching gospel doctrine, you're teaching gospel history. The unspoken theme of your lesson will be: Prop your eyelids open — this is going to be B-O-R-I-N-G.

But say that when you prepared your lesson, you realized that the Saints in Kirtland in the early 1830s, and the Prophet Joseph, had never seen a temple, let alone seen a picture of one, but they built the temple anyway. Now you might state your objective like this: *Today's lesson is about developing the faith to do things you may not know how to do.* And you'll introduce that objective by asking something like this: Has anyone been in a situation where you were asked to do something you didn't know how to do? When you ask that question, people will hesitate a little — pauses are standard protocol in gospel doctrine — but their minds will be churning, because they *have* done things they didn't know how to do, at home, at work, and in the Church. Then one or two brave people will raise their hands, and your lesson will take off, and all of a sudden you'll be talking not about facts or history, but about a gospel principle — faith — and how the members of your class have applied it.

Bottom line: A good objective will help you ask better questions. It will help you succinctly and memorably summarize the material in the manual, share the guidance you receive from the Spirit, and meet the spiritual needs of the members of your class. Inspired questions will help you address people's real needs.

THERE'S POWER IN SHARING EXPERIENCES, NOT JUST OPINIONS

A sidenote here: Almost every manual in the Church includes this admonition: *Encourage class members to share appropriate experiences that relate to the scriptural principles.* The key word there is *experiences.* Every lesson in the weekly "Come, Follow Me" outlines we use for home-centered learning asks questions designed to help you and your family share your experiences. Some examples:

- What tribulations have we experienced? How have these tribulations helped us to develop patience, experience, and hope?[34]

- Does your family know someone who could be described as "a cheerful giver"?[35]

- What experiences can your family share when they have "inquired of the Lord"?[36]

- Have a few "mighty" moments led to your change of heart, or has your conversion happened more gradually? [37]

If you ask experience-based questions, people will answer your questions, because everyone has had experiences that relate in some form to whatever topic you're addressing. A good discussion, which I think is a major goal of every teacher in every class in the Church, will result. But if you ask fact-based questions — What did Nephi say when he was commanded to build the boat? Where did the Sermon on the Mount take place? — your discussion will turn out like seventh grade math class.

Experience-based questions are how we talk when we're talking with our friends — and that kind of conversation is always interesting. *What did you do this weekend? Did you see the game? Have you ever got a warning instead of a speeding ticket, and do you think crying helps?* You don't talk with your friends and say: *What helped Nephi build the boat that took him and his family to the promised land? How long did it take the Saints to build the Kirtland Temple?* Conversations are interesting because there's give-and-take — and lessons with give-and-take are interesting, too. The best way to achieve that kind of discussion is to ask experience-based questions.

Remember this profound point in *Teaching in the Savior's Way:* "Each individual in your class is a rich source of testimony, insights, and experiences with living the gospel. Invite them to share with and lift each other."[38] How often should you do it? "As often as possible, invite learners to share their own stories and experiences."[39]

As you ask questions, here's related advice from *Teaching in the Savior's Way:* "Don't be afraid of silence. Good questions take time to answer. They require pondering, searching, and inspiration. The time you spend waiting for answers to a question can be a sacred time of pondering. Avoid the temptation to end this time too soon by answering your own question or moving on to something else."[40]

ASK YOURSELF: WHAT WILL PEOPLE REMEMBER ABOUT WHAT YOU SAY?

Here's one other thought to keep in mind when you're formulating an objective for a lesson. When the students in your class are home after church, sitting around the dinner table, what will they say when someone asks: What was your lesson on?

A related thought: The people in your class are more likely to remember what *they* say in class than what *you* say. That's human nature. (And even if they don't say anything, they'll remember what they thought about the things you said.) That's what they'll talk about when they discuss your lesson during Sunday dinner. Stephen R. Covey says in *Spiritual Roots of Spiritual Relations:* "Unless the learner is involved and dynamically participates in the learning process, very little, if any, learning (changed behavior) will result."[41] That's import-ant to remember, because it underscores the importance of asking the questions that facilitate a good discussion. The more people say in the lessons you teach, the more they'll remember about the lesson. Try it next Sunday: See what you say when someone asks you what your teacher in Sunday School or priesthood meeting or Relief Society talked about. Odds are that whatever you contributed to the lesson will be foremost in your mind.

But remember the lesson I learned from this experience. For two years I taught the same group of kids in Primary, first when they were 10 and then when they were 11. We got to know each other well. I loved them (most Sundays), and they loved me, as measured by their interest in teasing me. We had great discussions. I faithfully followed President McKay's three keys of effective teaching as I prepared and taught my lessons: I had an objective, I used examples, and I emphasized application. Often I posted the objective of each week's lesson on the board, so they could see it, then I'd reiterate it throughout the lesson.

And one Sunday I was talking with the dad of one of my students, a young man who was exceptionally bright and inquisitive. I told him his son asked good questions and listened closely; in fact he listened so well he often called me on any inconsistencies he noticed from week to week. I loved having him in our class. The boy was analytical almost to the point of being argumentative; he was outspoken, not afraid to disagree, and was totally engaged in our discussions.

His dad said: "*That's* interesting. Usually at Sunday dinner we ask him, 'What was your lesson on today?' And he always says: 'I don't remember.'"

Here's what that conversation taught me: Humility will always be one blessing of teaching in the kingdom.

CLARIFYING QUESTIONS: HAVE AN OBJECTIVE

Share your answers and see what others have posted at BetterTalksLDS.com.

1. In your last talk (or lesson), what was your objective? And was it simple, brief, and memorable?

2. How would you summarize the objective of one of your favorite talks? And how did that objective make a difference in the talk, and in your response?

3. When have you heard a talk when the speaker's objective was expressed directly, right up front — and how did it affect you?

4. How have you been impacted when people share experiences in gospel discussions?

5. When you look at your notes for your most recent lesson, what experience-based questions come to mind?

USE EXAMPLES

When I was 14 my mom and dad packed our family into our car and drove us two hours in church clothes to hear my cousin report his mission. My cousin, Bernard, had been a faithful missionary; he served in the Great Plains of the United States and southern Canada. During his talk he told the story of how he and his companion dropped by to visit a family they'd talked with who lived in a little farmhouse that sat by itself out in the middle of nowhere. They parked their truck at the end of the dirt driveway, then knocked on the door. The wife answered and invited them in. She was happy to see them; she'd been interested in their gospel message but her husband wasn't. As they talked they heard a truck drive up. The wife said: "Oh, no! It's my husband! He's probably been drinking, and he'll be mad you're here — he doesn't want me to talk with you any more. Quick — hide!"

They were in a one-room home. There was no inside bathroom. There was a bed in the corner, a small closet in another corner, and a kitchen table. Bernard and his companion considered crawling under the bed but there was no time. They raced to the closet, squeezed inside, and pulled the door shut. It was their only option.

They heard the man burst into the room. He was drunk. He'd seen the missionaries' truck. He called out that he had a knife — he was raving mad. "Where are the missionaries?" he said. "I know they're here! When I find them I'll make them pay for coming out here!"

The wife kept quiet. Bernard said: "Inside the closet, my companion and I did the only thing we could do. We said a prayer: 'Father in Heaven, please protect us.'"

He said: "We heard the man storming around the room, muttering and fuming. We heard him race over to look under the bed. We heard him approach the closet — it was the only other place to hide. We stood there, holding our breath, and waited for him to open the door. But he didn't. He just stood there for a few seconds, then he stumbled away and opened the outside door. We heard him stagger to his truck, get in, and drive away."

Bernard said: "Brothers and sisters, I *know* the Lord answers prayers."

I knew, too. His story — and the Spirit — really touched me that day, and forty-five years later, I still remember the story, and the spiritual impression, very clearly.

The best thing you can do once you've stated your objective — or *as* you state your objective — is to share examples that illustrate what you're talking about. Usually that means telling stories, then following your stories with a relevant scripture and with your testimony of the principle or lesson you're addressing.

Stories are often the most powerful, most memorable part of a talk or lesson. Here's proof: You may not remember the account in Luke 10 of the Lord's conversation with a lawyer who asked what's required to inherit eternal life — but you will remember the Lord's answer, which was the story of the Good Samaritan.

"The scriptures are primarily a collection of stories, given to us because God directed prophets to recount their experiences to His people," said Bruce C. Hafen during his service as a member of the First Quorum of Seventy. "In His desire to give us guidance about life, God could have given us a large rulebook or a series of grand philosophical essays. But He didn't. He gave us stories — about people like ourselves. Again and again the Book of Mormon writers tell us about some person's experience and say, 'And thus we see...'"[42]

"Stories are magic," says *Teaching, No Greater Call* — the long-time church teacher's manual. "No age is immune."[43] David O. McKay's advice: "Gather in experiences, and then illustrate each point. I think that is a message to every teacher."[44]

TWO STUDIES SHOW THE CONVINCING POWER OF STORIES

Here are two studies that make a scientific case for the power of stories.

The first is by business consultant and author Tom Peters in his best-selling book titled *Thriving on Chaos*. A group of MBA students at Stanford University were tested to measure their reactions to three forms of communication. One group of students — and note, these were business students, rooted and trained in analytics and statistics — was told a story that illustrated a company's commitment to avoiding layoffs during an economic downturn. Another group was given a collection of statistics that showed the company had a dramatically lower rate of layoffs than similar companies, and a third group got both the story and the statistics. So which group was most convinced that the company wasn't likely to lay off its employees when business was bad? "The story only group," says Peters, "even more than the group that got both the story and the statistics." The lesson, he says: "People live, reason, and are moved by symbols and stories...The best systems to ensure correct choices are 1) a clear vision, 2) sharing stories that illustrate how others, at all levels, have reacted to novel situations consistent with the vision."[45] He adds: "We are more influenced by stories than by data."[46]

Another study, conducted at Princeton University in 2010, involved neurological research and sounds like science fiction. A researcher told a fifteen-minute story — a funny-in-retrospect-but-not-at-the-time account of her high school prom, which included a fistfight between two boys who were competing for her attention and a car accident. While she recounted her experience, the brains of twelve test subjects were scanned by magnetic resonance imaging, which produces images of the internal organs and functions of the body. The result was described as shared "brain coupling" or a conjoining of the minds of the researcher who told the story and her test subjects. Professor Uri Hasson of the Princeton Neuroscience Institute said: "The results showed that not only did all of the listeners show similar brain activity during the story, the speaker and the listeners had very similar brain activity despite the fact that one person was producing language and the others were comprehending it."[47] Another reviewer described the results like this: "The broad application of magnetic resonance imaging and other brain scanning techniques, when combined with modern neuroscience, shows definitively why stories work in communications…Effective storytelling literally creates something the good Vulcan Mr. Spock could only fake in the movies and on TV: a *mind meld* between the storyteller and the audience."[48] In other words, when you tell a story, you connect with whoever's listening.

THREE KINDS OF EXAMPLES YOU CAN SHARE

Here are three of the main ways to share examples: 1) Tell personal stories, 2) Tell stories about someone else, and 3) Share parables.

THE FIRST WAY TO USE EXAMPLES: TELL PERSONAL STORIES

Since stories are magic — like the teacher's manual says — a personal story may be the best kind of example you can use. When my son was little, I remember a conversation during Sunday dinner about what we'd heard in church. Paul, who was about 7, said he especially liked one of the speakers in sacrament meeting. That impressed me because he was young enough that he usually preferred to color or play during the meeting. I asked him: Why did you like the talk? "He told stories," said Paul.

The author/business consultant Tom Peters made a similar point in his best-seller, *In Search of Excellence*. He said: Before computers were available, let alone personal, a man who owned a massive supercomputer wanted to know if it could be programmed to understand human thinking. The man typed into its interface: "Do you compute that you'll ever think like a human being?" The computer buzzed and whirred; its processors processed and its database hummed. Then the machine printed out its answer: "That reminds me of a story." Peters said: "This is indeed how people think."[49]

Of all the ways to use examples in a talk or lesson, telling a personal story is the most-used, and usually the most effective, way to illustrate your point. Remember the definition of a story: It's something that happened to you. Numerous passages in the scriptures encourage us to share the stories of our lives — and show their effectiveness. After Jesus cast out a legion of devils from a man in Gadarenes, he told the man: "Return to thine own house, and shew how great things God hath done unto thee." The man followed the Lord's counsel: "He went his way, and published throughout the whole city how great things Jesus had done unto him." And how did people respond to his personal story? Mark records: "All men did marvel."[50] When Paul and Barnabas were preaching in Antioch, "and had gathered the church together, they rehearsed all that God had done with them, and how he had opened the door of faith unto the Gentiles."[51]

And look at the powerful personal experience the Apostle Paul shared after he was arrested and cast into prison in Jerusalem: First he told where he was born and how he grew up (which is not unlike what a lot of speakers do in sacrament meeting), then he reviewed his background of persecuting the saints, and then he told this story: "And it came to pass, that, as I made my journey, and was come nigh unto Damascus about noon, suddenly there shone from heaven a great light round about me. And I fell unto the ground, and heard a voice saying unto me, Saul, Saul, why persecutest thou me? And I answered, Who art thou, Lord? And he said unto me, I am Jesus of Nazareth, whom thou persecutest." The scriptures are filled with similarly powerful personal experiences of the prophets and apostles — and so are the addresses the prophets and apostles share today. Jesus told one man: "Go home to thy friends, and tell them how great things the Lord had done for thee, and hath had compassion on thee."[52] It sounds like he was advising him what to say in testimony meeting, doesn't it? Or in sacrament meeting, next time he's assigned to talk.

Gordon B. Hinckley told personal stories so often that the whole church, if not the whole world, felt like they knew him. One example:

When I was a small boy in the first grade, I experienced what I thought was a rather tough day at school. I came home, walked in the house, threw my book on the kitchen table, and let forth an expletive that included the name of the Lord.

My mother was shocked. She told me quietly, but firmly, how wrong I was. She told me that I could not have words of that kind coming out of my mouth. She led me by the hand into the bath room, where she took from the shelf a clean washcloth, put it under the faucet, then generously coated it with soap. She said, "We'll have to wash out your mouth." She told me to open it, and I did so reluctantly. Then she rubbed the soapy washcloth around my tongue and teeth. I sputtered and fumed and felt like swearing again, but I didn't. I rinsed and rinsed my mouth, but it was a long while before the soapy taste was gone. In fact, whenever I think of that experience, I can still taste the soap.

The lesson was worthwhile. I think I can say that I have tried to avoid using the name of the Lord in vain since that day.[53]

President Hinckley's experience is so vivid you can almost taste the soap — and it's easy to remember his lesson: Bad language leaves a bad taste in your mouth.

Here's more encouragement to share personal stories, starting with a church leadership handbook, which says: "Teachers and class members are encouraged to share insights, feelings, and experiences that relate to principles in the lesson…This helps teachers and class members strengthen friendships and see how gospel principles apply to daily life."[54] *Teaching, No Greater Call*, says: "Relating personal experiences can have a powerful influence in helping others live gospel principles. When you tell about what you have experienced yourself, you act as a living witness of gospel truths. If you speak truthfully and with pure intent, the Spirit will confirm the truth of your message in the hearts of those you teach."[55] I previously mentioned this line that's in almost every lesson manual in the Church: "Encourage class members to share appropriate experiences that relate to the scriptural principles." And Bruce R. McConkie said: "Perhaps the perfect pattern in presenting faith-promoting stories is to teach what is found in the scriptures and then to put a seal of living reality upon it by telling a similar and equivalent thing that has happened in our dispensation and to our people and — most ideally — to us as individuals."[56]

And don't think that stories are something you should just use when you teach kids or that they're a crutch when you don't have more powerful content. They can be the *point* of your content. Brent James, MD, a nationally renowned, Harvard-trained physician who speaks extensively to health system leaders and physicians, said: "You know what you do to teach adult learners effectively? You tell stories, and then you pull out principles the stories illustrate. Your effectiveness as an instructor of adult learners depends on how many good stories you have."[57] Again: Fill your talks with stories — then share your testimony of the principles or lessons they teach.

Bruce C. Hafen of the First Quorum of Seventy said, "Our own testimonies are true and often powerful stories that capture in vivid detail how the Lord blesses us, protects us, changes us, and helps us to overcome. Nothing brings the Spirit into a conversation or a classroom more than hearing people bear honest testimony, not so much by exhortation as by just telling the story of their personal experience."[58]

THE BENEFITS OF PERSONAL STORIES

Why are personal stories so effective when you give a talk or teach a lesson — and how do they benefit the people you're addressing (and you)?

1. STORIES ARE CREDIBLE. That's because they're about something you *did*, not something you thought about or Googled or read. The people who listen to you are more likely to believe you when they know you've tried to live what you're teaching. What you've done carries greater weight in their minds than what you say. "You teach what you are," said Elder Neal A. Maxwell in a 1982 address. "…If our discipleship is serious, it will show."[59] Joseph Fielding McConkie repeated the idea in a speech about the principles upon which his father, Bruce R. McConkie, built his life: "Competence as a witness is predicated upon empirical knowledge — that which you have experienced."[60]

2. STORIES ARE INTERESTING. When we talk with our family or friends we share personal experiences: What did you learn at school today? What happened at work? Likewise, when you're telling a story in a talk or a lesson, your talk is more like conversation than preaching. People sense that, and they prefer conversations to preaching; it strengthens their connection to you and to the principle you're teaching. Telling stories reflects Mahatma Gandhi's sweet and simple advice: "An ounce of practice is worth more than tons of preaching."[61]

3. STORIES ARE MEMORABLE. The details of a story help people remember what you say. Illustrating a gospel principle with a story enhances your listeners' ability to retain information — and as you tell a story, then relate it to the principle you're illustrating, you create the repetition that builds retention. A one-word example: Visualize Dieter F. Uchtdorf speaking in conference, then think of one word — *airplane* — and your memories will warm your heart (and make you smile).

4. STORIES ARE EASY TO TELL. Telling something that happened to you means you can rely more on your memory than your notes — which will enhance the emotional connection between you and the people who are listening. When you tell stories, you're likely to be less nervous and more confident and relaxed as you speak. Again, you're not preaching, which is probably an uncomfortable setting for you; you're telling your story in the way you normally talk when you're with your family or friends or colleagues, which is natural and comfortable.

4. STORIES ARE A PROFOUND WAY TO SHARE THINGS ONLY YOU CAN SHARE. No one else has had the experiences you've had. You're the only person who can share them. If you tell a story Nephi or Jeffrey Holland or David Bednar or Sheri Dew told, I guarantee you: They can tell it better than you can. But when you tell a personal story, you're inviting the people who are listening onto the sacred ground of your memories. You're investing trust in them and strengthening your connection with them. In *Spiritual Roots of Human Relations*, Stephen Covey said when we're emotionally open, we run the risk we may be changed. And whether we're speaking or listening, isn't changing the point of our talks and lessons at church?[62]

Maybe you noticed: Many of the benefits of sharing personal experiences have a theme. They build *connections* — between you and the people who are listening to you, and often, between you and them and the Lord's

Spirit. They fulfill a mandate Gordon B. Hinckley shared with gospel teachers in a 1965 conference talk: "Your students deserve more than your knowledge," he said. "They deserve and hunger for your inspiration. They want the warm glow of personal relationships. This has always been the hallmark of a great teacher."[63]

THREE EXAMPLES OF PERSONAL STORIES

Here are three delightfully different examples of the kind of stories that provide that warm glow — and which are credible, interesting, memorable, easy to tell, and completely, wonderfully personal. First, one of my close friends is Nathan Jarvis, a former stake president from Olathe, Kansas, who took a ski vacation to Salt Lake City with his family several years ago. He drove from the city up the canyon to a ski resort by himself early one morning, and as he drove, he engaged in a mental exercise he enjoyed when he had uninterrupted time to think: He constructed a talk in his mind. That morning he focused on the subject of profanity. He said after about 45 minutes of driving, he arrived at the ski resort, opened the trunk of his car — and found he'd left his ski boots back in the city. "Before I realized it," he said, "I had a new anecdote for my talk."[64]

Second, another friend, Heather Barth, shared this sacred story: "On September 10, 1980, early on a very rainy morning, I found myself kneeling across the altar of a sealing room in the Salt Lake Temple. Across from me knelt a young man I had grown to love over the last 11 months. He held me by the right hand and smiled at me with his eyes. My grandfather stood to our side and spoke to us as he officiated at our sealing. The room was beautiful and our parents were looking on with love. At that moment I had the strongest witness of the Holy Ghost I had ever felt then or since. A warm feeling came to my chest, a literal 'burning in my bosom.' It was hot and strong and like a bolt of lightning to my heart. Immediately to my mind came the words: 'You are in the right place, at the right time, and with the right man.' I have known from that moment on that my Heavenly Father loves me and that Peter Hans Barth is my eternal companion. I have a testimony that as we make correct choices the Holy Ghost will witness to us of their correctness."[65]

And third, this example from Henry B. Eyring powerfully illustrates the idea that telling personal stories allows you to share impressions, memories, feelings, and lessons that only you can share:

The afternoon my mother died, we went to the family home from the hospital. We sat quietly in the darkened living room for a while. Dad excused himself and went to his bedroom. He was gone for a few minutes. When he walked back into the living room, there was a smile on his face. He said that he'd been concerned for mother. During the time he had gathered her things from her hospital room and thanked the staff for being so kind to her, he thought of her going into the spirit world just minutes after her death. He was afraid she would be lonely if there was no one to meet her.

He had gone to his bedroom to ask his Heavenly Father to have someone greet Mildred, his wife and my mother. He said that he had been told in answer to his prayer that his mother had met his sweetheart. I smiled at that too. Grandma Eyring was not very tall. I had a clear picture of her rushing through the crowd, her short legs moving rapidly on her mission to meet my mother.

Dad surely didn't intend at that moment to teach me about prayer, but he did.[66]

THE SECOND WAY TO USE EXAMPLES:
TELL STORIES ABOUT SOMEONE ELSE

Sometimes another person's experience will fit better in a talk or lesson than a personal experience. Sometimes that experience will be from the scriptures — but remember Nephi's advice to *liken the scriptures unto yourself*,[67] which means to share personal stories that illustrate scriptural principles. Again, our own personal experiences are more credible, more interesting, more memorable, and easier to tell — and they allow you to share things only you can share.

I think that's worth remembering, and so is this: Sometimes telling someone else's story is the best thing you can do. David Meek, one of my close friends, gave a talk in sacrament meeting in January 2016 about the reasons why we do the things we do. He used a historical story, not a personal story, to introduce his theme: He talked briefly about Kenesaw Mountain Landis, a federal judge in Illinois in the early 1900s, who was appointed commissioner of baseball in 1920, shortly after eight players from the Chicago White Sox were indicted and tried for conspiring with a group of gamblers to throw the 1919 World Series. The players were acquitted in court, but the commissioner, who had absolute power over professional baseball in America, banned the players for life. David asked a question — why did the commissioner ban the eight players? — then he quoted Judge Landis:

> Baseball is something more than a game to an American boy; it is his training field for life's work. Destroy his faith in its squareness and honesty and you have destroyed something more; you have planted suspicion of all things in his heart.

The congregation — which included me — was intrigued. We were immersed in what David was saying and ready to go wherever his talk would take us. His historical story really worked. He told me afterward: "I could tell people were really listening."[68]

Here's a personal David Meek story, which I used in a talk — another example of using an example that's not a personal experience. Some background: David is my tennis buddy; he and I have played almost every Saturday morning for 30 years. Although "play" may be the wrong verb; the older we get, the longer we sit and talk between sets. David and I have had several similar callings in the Church, and for a number of years we both taught gospel doctrine in our different wards. Our lessons were perfectly aligned; whatever lesson I was teaching, he'd taught the week before. It was a huge blessing to talk with David on Saturday morning at tennis. We'd sit down during our breaks and drink water and ask: *How did you keep people interested in Isaiah? What principles did you find in the text? What stories did you tell?* His answers were terrific; he was a wonderful resource. Everyone who teaches should have a friend like David Meek, especially during Old Testament year.

One year I was asked to talk in our ward on Mother's Day, and as I pondered and prayed about what I should say, I felt an impression: *Tell the story David told you.* That didn't make sense. A week or two previously David had told me about an aggravating experience he'd had that spring, but his story didn't relate to mothers. I kept looking for other material for my talk, but my thoughts kept returning to David's story. The impression persisted. *Tell that story.*

David had experienced a major disagreement with a man who'd provided some professional services for him. David wasn't happy with the services and he pointed out his dissatisfaction. He was calm and thought he was reasonable in sharing his complaints. He was the customer, he'd paid for the services, and he didn't get what he paid for. He was disappointed. But the man he was dealing with — who we'll call Kirk, which is appropriate, since it rhymes with *jerk* — blew up. Not only was he not going to apologize for the poor service or make some kind of amends, but he was angry with David for sharing his feedback. He railed on David, and David raised his voice in response. Their anger boiled, then Kirk stepped close enough to David to bump into him. They were right on the lip of a fistfight. David could tell that's what Kirk was pushing for — and it wasn't a good idea: Kirk was a great big guy, taller and heavier than David. David thought: *If this comes to a fight, he'll kill me.* He stepped back.

Kirk told David: *Get out of here — you're not welcome as my customer any more!*

David said: *I can agree with that. Don't worry — I won't be back.* He turned and walked out. They were both shaking; they were steaming mad.

A couple of days later, on a Sunday, David ran into a member of the board that oversees Kirk's company. The board member was David's friend; they lived in the same ward. David recounted his experience, and the board member knew all about Kirk. He said Kirk had had problems with other customers, much like the problem he had with David. The board member said: *Kirk has a history of being belligerent, and in fact he may have a drinking problem.* The man encouraged David to write a summary of what had happened. Documenting the experience, said the board member, would mean the encounter would be part of Kirk's personnel file and it would enable his manager to follow up, and probably fire him. Kirk deserved it. The board member told David: *You're not the only person who's upset with how he's treated you. I'm sure he deserves to be fired, and your documentation will help us do it.* David thought: *Good. That's what he deserves.*

But a day or two later, he reconsidered. Instead of filing a complaint, he called the company and asked to speak to Kirk. When Kirk came to the phone, David said: *I'm sorry. I lost my temper; I was out of line. Please forgive me.*

There was a pause on the line. David told me: "Kirk almost cried. He had to get control of himself before he could say anything. He said, 'No, *I* was wrong. I lost my cool; *you* need to forgive *me.*'" Sitting by a tennis court one sunny Saturday morning, David's voice choked with emotion when he told me that story — and I felt what I've often felt when David and I talk about holy subjects: I felt the Spirit of the Lord.

A week later, after I'd been convinced I should tell that story in my Mother's Day talk, I asked David's permission to share it, and I asked: *Did your mom happen to influence your response?* He started to say no, his mom's been gone for many years. But then he said: "Yes. When I look back at my life, my dad taught me how to initiate conflict, and my mom taught me how to resolve it." I quoted that comment in my talk, then I segued into my objective: *When we think about the influences that help us follow the Lord and earn the peace he gives to those who keep his commandments, mothers — and the women in our lives — are at the top of almost everyone's list.* I quoted Boyd K. Packer, who said: "You will know if you know me at all that Sister Packer has been the major influence in everything I do."[69] I don't know why I was supposed to tell David's story that Sunday. But I do know: I felt the warmth and the power of the Lord's Spirit when I talked about how David had forgiven Kirk, and sharing the Spirit is the reason why we speak.

If you need another source of stories about people who've lived gospel principles, look at church history. Jeffrey R. Holland provides a terrific example in his book *Trusting Jesus*. He tells the story of a group of men sent by Brigham Young to rescue the members of the Willie handcart company in the harsh winter of 1856 near Rocky Ridge, Wyoming. The rescue party found the survivors at Martin's Cove — starving, freezing, sick, and dying. Dan Jones, a recent convert who'd been called as one of the rescuers, said later that they were in a state of distress more anguishing than anything he'd ever witnessed before or since. The rescuers revived the handcart survivors, then one party of men accompanied them to Salt Lake City while another party stayed in a fort in Devil's Gate, Wyoming, to safeguard their possessions until spring.

While the rescuers waited out the bitter winter, they soon faced conditions as harrowing as the people they'd rescued. They ran out of food. Their attempts to hunt were unsuccessful. They were reduced to eating cattle hides, which made them sick. Brother Jones recorded: "We asked the Lord to bless our stomachs and adapt them to this food. We hadn't the faith to ask him to bless the cowhide." When the hides were gone they ate the soles of their moccasins and the leather wrappings used to hold their wagons together.

But did they think of abandoning their post? "There was not money enough on earth to have hired me to stay," Brother Jones wrote years later. "But I remembered my assertion that any of us would stay if called upon. I could not [break my word]."

Then things got worse. A gang of apostates rode to up to the fort, intent on stealing anything of value left behind by the handcart pioneers. Dan Jones stepped out to accost them. Elder Holland tells the story like this:

Brother Jones came out of the barricade alone, walking some 30 yards toward his opponents. As they started to move in, he placed his hand on his pistol and told them to halt. "I explained our situation," he said. "I told them that we were custodians of the goods that had been left there."

...[Dan said] President Brigham Young had called them to this assignment, and they were determined to fulfill their responsibility. Their allegiance to God and His prophet was the only allegiance they had in this circumstance, and it was an allegiance they were determined to maintain.

As the marauders again started to make their move, Dan Jones said something like this: "We've been here all winter eating cow's gristle and rawhide, nearly freezing to death to take care of those emigrants' possessions. If you think you can take this fort after what we have given to stay here, just try it. Now I dare you to take one more step toward those goods."

There was a deadly silence. No one moved. It was a breathless moment. Then the enemy leader said, "Dan Jones, I think you are (blankety blank) fool enough to die before you would give up those goods."

Brother Jones said, "Thank you. I am glad you understand me so correctly."

Brother Holland adds: "That story then goes on to a happy ending. The enemies rode away empty-handed."[70]

One thought in conclusion: As you search for examples to illustrate the topic you're addressing, the Spirit will guide you. But you have to make the search — and you're usually wise to start by considering your own experiences. Elder Gene R. Cook said in *Teaching By The Spirit:* "One reason why personal experiences are so effective is that they have touched our hearts — and when we speak of things that we feel deeply, it is more likely that we'll be able to touch the hearts of others. If you read a lesson and tell a story in someone else's words, it won't have the same impact...It is easier for us to apply a truth if we can see it in action in someone else's life. And it is easier to commit to live a truth if we can feel the Spirit through those experiences of other people."[71]

Two overarching thoughts to take away when you think about telling stories: 1) Sharing your own personal experiences is the best way to use examples in your talks and lesson — 2) Unless the Lord's Spirit directs you to do otherwise.

THE THIRD WAY TO USE EXAMPLES: SHARE PARABLES

Everyone who's read the scriptures understands the power of parables. Dictionary.com defines a parable like this: "A short allegorical story designed to illustrate or teach some truth, religious principle, or moral lesson; a statement or comment that conveys a meaning indirectly by the use of comparison, analogy, or the like." Richard Lloyd Anderson, a professor of history and ancient scripture at BYU, describes them like this: "Earthly stories with heavenly meanings."[72] Parables comprise many of the best-known and most-quoted parts of the scriptural canon. Wikipedia says:

> Jesus' parables are seemingly simple and memorable stories, often with imagery, and all convey messages. Scholars have commented that although these parables seem simple, the messages they convey are deep, and central to the teachings of Jesus. Christian authors view them not as mere similitudes which serve the purpose of illustration, but as internal analogies in which nature becomes a witness for the spiritual world...

In the modern age, even among those who know little of the Bible, the parables of Jesus remain some of the best-known stories in the world.

The stories you tell when you follow David O. McKay's advice to use examples — including your own personal stories or stories about someone else — are parables in the sense that they're allegories designed to illustrate or teach a spiritual principle. But parables are different than stories; usually they're simpler, sometimes they don't have an anecdotal narrative, and most often they require some creative thought. It takes real imagination to think of something in the physical world that illustrates something in the spiritual world — and there's a paradox that accompanies their creation: Because parables are simple, concocting one often requires intellectual heavy lifting. They're not easy to devise.

The parable of the sower is a great example. Here it is as recounted in Mark 4: 2-20:

And (Jesus) taught them many things by parables, and said unto them in his doctrine, Hearken; Behold, there went out a sower to sow: And it came to pass, as he sowed, some fell by the way side, and the fowls of the air came and devoured it up.

And some fell on stony ground, where it had not much earth; and immediately it sprang up, because it had no depth of earth: But when the sun was up, it was scorched; and because it had no root, it withered away.

And some fell among thorns, and the thorns grew up, and choked it, and it yielded no fruit.

And other fell on good ground, and did yield fruit that sprang up and increased; and brought forth, some thirty, and some sixty, and some an hundred.

And he said unto them, He that hath ears to hear, let him hear. And when he was alone, they that were about him with the twelve asked of him the parable.

And he said unto them, Unto you it is given to know the mystery of the kingdom of God: but unto them that are without, all these things are done in parables: That seeing they may see, and not perceive; and hearing they may hear, and not understand; lest at any time they should be converted, and their sins should be forgiven them.

And he said unto them, Know ye not this parable? and how then will ye know all parables?

The sower soweth the word. And these are they by the way side, where the word is sown; but when they have heard, Satan cometh immediately, and taketh away the word that was sown in their hearts.

And these are they likewise which are sown on stony ground; who, when they have heard the word, immediately receive it with gladness; And have no root in themselves, and so endure but for a time: afterward, when affliction or persecution ariseth for the word's sake, immediately they are offended.

And these are they which are sown among thorns; such as hear the word, And the cares of this world, and the deceitfulness of riches, and the lusts of other things entering in, choke the word, and it becometh unfruitful.

And these are they which are sown on good ground; such as hear the word, and receive it, and bring forth fruit, some thirtyfold, some sixty, and some an hundred.

A confession: When I started to read the scriptures when I was young, I'd read how the disciples repeatedly asked the Lord: *Why do you speak in parables? We don't know what you're saying!* And I'd think: *Are you kidding? That's the most understandable part of what the scriptures say!*

Boyd K. Packer included a wonderful parable as part of a personal story he shared at a seminar for new mission presidents in 1982[73]:

We do not learn spiritual things in exactly the same way we learn other things that we know...I have learned that it requires a special attitude both to teach and to learn spiritual things. There are some things you know, or may come to know, that you will find quite difficult to explain to others. I am very certain it was meant to be that way.

I will tell you of an experience I had before I was a General Authority which affected me profoundly. I sat on a plane next to a professed atheist who pressed his disbelief in God so urgently that I bore my testimony to him. "You are wrong," I said. "There is a God. I know He lives!"

He protested, "You don't know. Nobody knows that! You can't know it!" When I would not yield, the atheist, who was an attorney, asked perhaps the ultimate question on the subject of testimony. "All right," he said in a sneering, condescending way, "you say you know. Tell me how you know."

When I attempted to answer, even though I held advanced academic degrees, I was helpless to communicate.

...When I used the words *Spirit* and *witness*, the atheist responded, "I don't know what you are talking about." The words *prayer*, *discernment*, and *faith* were equally meaningless to him. "You see," he said, "you don't really know. If you did, you would be able to tell me how you know."

I felt, perhaps, that I had borne my testimony to him unwisely and was at a loss as to what to do. Then came the experience! Something came into my mind. And I mention here a statement of the Prophet Joseph Smith: "A person may profit by noticing the first intimation of the spirit of revelation; for instance, when you feel pure intelligence flowing into you, it may give you sudden strokes of ideas...and thus by learning the Spirit of God and understanding it, you may grow into the principle of revelation, until you become perfect in Christ Jesus."

Such an idea came into my mind and I said to the atheist, "Let me ask if you know what salt tastes like."

"Of course I do," was his reply.

"When did you taste salt last?"

"I just had dinner on the plane."

"You just think you know what salt tastes like," I said.

He insisted, "I know what salt tastes like as well as I know anything."

"If I gave you a cup of salt and a cup of sugar and let you taste them both, could you tell the salt from the sugar?"

"Now you are getting juvenile," was his reply. "Of course I could tell the difference. I know what salt tastes like. It is an everyday experience — I know it as well as I know anything."

"Then," I said, "assuming that I have never tasted salt, explain to me just what it tastes like."

After some thought, he ventured, "Well-I-uh, it is not sweet and it is not sour."

"You've told me what it isn't, not what it is."

After several attempts, of course, he could not do it. He could not convey, in words alone, so ordinary an experience as tasting salt. I bore testimony to him once again and said, "I know there is a God. You ridiculed that testimony and said that if I did know, I would be able to tell you exactly how I know. My friend, spiritually speaking, I have tasted salt. I am no more able to convey to you in words how this knowledge has come than you are to tell me what salt tastes like. But I say to you again, there is a God! He does live! And just because you don't know, don't try to tell me that I don't know, for I do!"

Another parable with a vivid narrative structure is part of an article Gordon B. Hinckley wrote for the *Ensign* in 2000. "I have a simple story I would like to recount," he said. "It is something of a parable. I do not have the name of the author." He said:

Years ago there was a little one-room schoolhouse in the mountains of Virginia where the boys were so rough that no teacher had been able to handle them.

A young, inexperienced teacher applied, and the old director scanned him and asked: "Young fellow, do you know that you are asking for an awful beating? Every teacher that we have had here for years has had to take one."

"I will risk it," he replied.

The first day of school came, and the teacher appeared for duty. One big fellow named Tom whispered: "I won't need any help with this one. I can lick him myself."

The teacher said, "Good morning, boys, we have come to conduct school." They yelled and made fun at the top of their voices. "Now, I want a good school, but I confess that I do not know how unless you help me. Suppose we have a few rules. You tell me, and I will write them on the blackboard."

"One fellow yelled, "No stealing! " Another yelled, "On time." Finally, 10 rules appeared on the blackboard.

"Now," said the teacher, "a law is not good unless there is a penalty attached. What shall we do with one who breaks the rules?"

"Beat him across the back 10 times without his coat on," came the response from the class.

"That is pretty severe, boys. Are you sure that you are ready to stand by it?" Another yelled, "I second the motion," and the teacher said, "All right, we will live by them! Class, come to order!"

In a day or so, "Big Tom" found that his lunch had been stolen. The thief was located — a little hungry fellow, about 10 years old.

"We have found the thief and he must be punished according to your rule — 10 stripes across the back. Jim, come up here!" the teacher said.

The little fellow, trembling, came up slowly with a big coat fastened up to his neck and pleaded, "Teacher, you can lick me as hard as you like, but please, don't take my coat off!"

"Take your coat off," the teacher said. "You helped make the rules!"

"Oh, teacher, don't make me!" He began to unbutton, and what did the teacher see? The boy had no shirt on, and revealed a bony little crippled body.

"How can I whip this child?" he thought. "But I must, I must do something if I am to keep this school." Everything was quiet as death.

"How come you aren't wearing a shirt, Jim?"

He replied, "My father died and my mother is very poor. I have only one shirt and she is washing it today, and I wore my brother's big coat to keep me warm."

The teacher, with rod in hand, hesitated. Just then Big Tom jumped to his feet and said, "Teacher, if you don't object, I will take Jim's licking for him."

"Very well, there is a certain law that one can become a substitute for another. Are you all agreed?"

Off came Tom's coat, and after five strokes the rod broke! The teacher bowed his head in his hands and thought, "How can I finish this awful task?" Then he heard the class sobbing, and what did he see? Little Jim had reached up and caught Tom with both arms around his neck. "Tom, I'm sorry that I stole your lunch, but I was awful hungry. Tom, I will love you till I die for taking my licking for me! Yes, I will love you forever!"

To lift a phrase from this simple story, Jesus, my Redeemer, has taken "my licking for me" and yours for you. Declared the prophet Isaiah: "Surely he hath borne our griefs, and carried our sorrows... He was wounded for our transgressions, he was bruised for our iniquities: the chastisement of our peace was upon him; and with his stripes we are healed."[74]

Using a metaphor — which uses one item to describe something else — can be a kind of succinct parable that makes your topic come alive. Martin Luther King, Jr., used that device unforgettably in his address titled, "I Have a Dream," which was heralded as the most powerful American speech of the 20th century.[75] Copyright law prevents me from sharing his manuscript, but look up his speech — and look specifically for his metaphor about trying to cash a bad check at the bank of justice.

Here's another example. Bradley R. Wilcox used this relevant metaphor in his October 2021 conference talk: "Life is like a cross-country road trip. We can't reach our destination on one tank of gas. We must refill the tank over and over. Taking the sacrament is like pulling into the gas station. As we repent and renew our covenants, we pledge our willingness to keep the commandments, and God and Christ bless us with the Holy Spirit. In short, we promise to press forward on our journey, and God and Christ promise to refill the tank."[76]

James E. Talmage recounted the benefits of using parables in *Jesus the Christ*. He describes Jesus's charge to his disciplines: "They should be ready, like well-taught teachers, to bring, from the store-house of their souls, treasures of truth both old and new for the edification of the world." Elder Talmage said the effectiveness of telling stories is a "psychological fact," and said: "The incidents of an impressive though simple story will live, even in minds which for the time being are incapable of comprehending any meaning beyond that of the commonplace story itself." And he added: "The parables of the New Testament, spoken by the Teacher of teachers, are of such beauty, simplicity, and effectiveness as to stand unparalleled in literature."[77]

Thomas S. Monson adds this endorsement: "Jesus made parables a part of nearly every teaching situation. So often did he use this teaching device that evangelists recorded at one point that 'without a parable spake he not unto them.' Jesus said he used parables in teaching because they conveyed to the hearer religious truth exactly in proportion to the hearer's faith and intelligence. To the unlearned, the parable had story interest and some teaching value. To the spiritual, it conveyed much more, including the mysteries or secrets of the kingdom of heaven. Thus the parable is suited alike to simple and learned. It teaches all people to find divine truth in common things."[78]

HOW CAN YOU COME UP WITH STORIES FOR YOUR TALKS AND LESSONS IF YOUR MIND DOESN'T WORK THAT WAY?

Everything reminds me of a story — that's how my mind works. When a teacher asks a question in priesthood meeting or Sunday School, my mind flashes to experiences that may relate. That may be a genetic thing: My dad was an accountant and my mom was a writer, and I got all of mom's genes and none of dad's. But a lot of people say: I just can't come up with any good experiences. They're too hard to think of.

Gene R. Cook described that challenge — and the solution — in *Teaching By the Spirit*: "Some people have said to me, 'Well, Elder Cook, it's easy for you to tell stories. You have so many great experiences. But I don't even know one single story from my own life.' To them I say, 'Well, maybe you don't, but the Lord does. You've had a lot of spiritual experiences, but you may not have recognized them. The Lord can pull them out of you if you believe that he will, if you will pray for the blessing, and if you practice doing it. Sometimes you can take the simplest experience that happened only an hour before and teach a powerful lesson from it — if you're being observant. Learn to observe all the 'little things' going on around you, and you will find you have many more experiences and stories to tell."[79]

Here are five ways to find personal stories for your talks and lessons:

FIRST, PONDER AND PRAY TO THINK OF THE RIGHT EXPERIENCES (AND START PREPARING EARLY). Starting to think of personal experiences a week or two before you're speaking will help; so will asking your family members and friends for ideas. Coming up with the right stories may be difficult, but if you invest the effort, you'll find what you're looking for. Alma 29:4 — God grants unto us according to our desires — tells you your mental energies will be rewarded. And the Lord will guide you; the Spirit will help you as you prepare your talk or lesson. Elder Cook promised: "If you're sensitive to the Spirit, you will find that the Lord will tell you what to share and when."[80]

SECOND, LOOK FOR EVERYDAY EXPERIENCES (NOT MAJOR DRAMATIC INCIDENTS). Remember the definition of a story: It's something that happened to you. The fact that you've read this far into this book says you're interested in finding personal experiences for your talks and lessons. So just pay attention to what happens to you. Watch for conversations and experiences that reflect gospel principles or life lessons. They're there. You just have to notice them.

"As we seek for a mind and heart open to receive heavenly direction by the power of the Holy Ghost, then some of the greatest instructions that we can receive and many of the most powerful warnings that can safeguard us will originate in our own ordinary experiences," Elder David A. Bednar said in a general conference address. "Powerful parables are contained in both the scriptures and in our daily lives."[81]

One problem I saw during my last stint as a gospel doctrine teacher: Typically we choose dramatic experiences to illustrate the principles we're talking about — but life isn't dramatic. Too often I go looking for a powerful, miraculous experience when I teach; I want a story about the Red Sea parting or angels appearing. But that's not the way life works, and it's not the way the Lord usually works. Stephen Covey said in *Spiritual Roots of Human Relations:* "I fear that in our study of God and his dealings with us, we focus on the special, the sudden, the dramatic, and overlook his silent, natural, gradual workings within the breast of each individual who surrenders his will to a higher will."[82]

An example of a small but instructive experience: When my daughter Emily was about four, one Sunday at dinner we asked her what her lesson in Primary had been on. She lifted up one of her white Sunday shoes with its little buckle so everyone could see it. She said, "Our lesson was, my teacher says these are the prettiest shoes she's ever seen!" I loved that answer — and loved the teacher for expressing such a meaningful sentiment to Em. I don't know what the lesson was about, but the teacher was teaching 1 John 4:19: Emily loved her because she first loved Emily.

THIRD, KEEP A JOURNAL. One reason why so many leaders of the Church have great stories when they speak is because they have great journals. In my journal, which I've kept since my mission, I don't write every day or every week, and sometimes not every month. But I do record experiences I want to remember. I keep my journal on my computer in my den, and when I'm looking for a story for a lesson or a talk, it's easy to open the file and do a key word search: I've searched for "Spirit" or "Prayer" or "Melissa's wise advice" or other topics; a couple of key strokes and I have three or four options, all personal stories, all ready to use.

One example: On September 1, 2013, I wrote about a family dinner we hosted at our house on a Sunday evening, after which little Spencer, our grandson, filled up his squirt gun and walked toward me. But I made like a gazelle to Spence's lion; I took off. Spencer chased me around the backyard and tried to corner me without success, then altered his strategy, which I recorded like this:

Spencer: Grandpa, let me show dis to you!
Grandpa: No — you'll squirt me!
Spencer: Me won't squirt you!

What would you do? Spence was not quite three at the time; pure, sweet, energetic, and joyful. I came close and bent down to check out the squirt gun. But it was a trap. He *blasted* me.

Grandpa: I thought you said you wouldn't squirt me!
Spencer: Me change my mind!

Gene R. Cook said: "I've found that many experiences with my family have been of great benefit to others, and I believe strongly in recording in some detail my key experiences week after week. I have learned, as have many others, that if I do not record them when they occur, the impact of the experiences or the feelings that attended them are soon lost. However, if I record them and remember them, I can use them to help others."[83]

FOURTH, READ THE SCRIPTURES...AND LIKEN THEM UNTO YOURSELF. Here's an effective pattern to follow: 1) Use a scripture, 2) Tell a story, and 3) Bear testimony. The scripture introduces the topic you're addressing, the story explains how it works, and your testimony adds a spiritual charge that can carry it into people's hearts. Each step reinforces the others; they harness the principle that repetition builds retention — and each step will help you not only be interesting, but be a vessel of the Lord's Spirit.

This passage in Moroni 6:5 is an example of likening the scriptures unto ourselves: "And the church did meet together oft, to fast and to pray, and to speak one with another concerning the welfare of their souls." To me that's a *perfect* description of the first personal priesthood interview I had as a new bishop. I'd only been serving about a month, and going to visit with our stake president made me nervous. I didn't know what to expect, and because I was so new in the calling, I didn't feel like I had a good grasp of what our ward was like. So I approached the PPI like it was a mid-term exam, and I did some cramming: I reviewed our average sacrament meeting attendance, our home teaching rates, our percent of endowed members with current temple recommends, our number of families and numbers of young people. My appointment with the stake president — Jim Parkin — began at almost 11 one night, and I walked into his office with my head buzzing.

But my study was a waste of time. President Parkin — who's one of the most effective leaders I know — asked only five or six questions. The first one was: How are you doing? All of the rest were about members of our ward: How's Matt Matthews? How's Jane Jeffers? How's Roscoe Robertson? That was all he wanted to know. Our wise stake president reflected Moroni's counsel: *We spoke one with another concerning the welfare of the souls* of the members of my ward. I loved that focus, and it was a great lesson to me as a young bishop about what my focus should be.

FIFTH, READ, PERIOD. Church books, biographies, family histories, and almost everything you read will have stories and examples that can relate to a gospel principle you'll be talking about. "Uplifting quotations from wholesome literature can…enrich a lesson," says *Teaching in the Savior's Way*.[84]

I remember being impressed with a story in *Sports Illustrated* in 2006 about Steve Wallace, the offensive tackle for the San Francisco 49ers, and the exhaustive efforts he made to study the tendencies of the defensive ends and linebackers he battled during his career in the NFL. The details of the article recounted how Steve had an inferiority complex; he thought he wasn't as big, as strong, or as fast as the players he faced on the other side of the line — and he was chronically worried about losing his job. He looked at the huge, fast, aggressive players he was supposed to block and thought: "You go by me and my family goes hungry."

So he studied film before each week's game and made intricate adjustments to help him fulfill his assignments and keep his job. He learned exactly, to the inch, where to line up before a snap, he checked out the referees of each game and what they were known to focus on, and he watched for subtle hints that indicated whether his opponents were going to try to run over him or around him on their way to his quarterback. And thus he learned where to place his feet and his hands when he was under attack by an opposing player, how to adjust the angle and timing of his blocks, and when to plant his feet.

One October Sunday when I was teaching gospel doctrine, I read a brief excerpt from the article about how Wallace's meticulous preparations helped him succeed. The lesson was an introduction to the book of Isaiah, and my point was: People who can see more than you can see — people who know what's coming — can enhance your life if you'll listen to them. BYU's Steve Young was one of the 49er quarterbacks Wallace protected; clearly that strengthened the doctrinal link. To me, the example turned out to be gripping, and after the lesson I asked my wife how well it went over. She said: "Well…I don't think the sisters were as blown away as the brothers." (The *Sports Illustrated* account, by the way, was taken from an excellent book called *The Blind Side*, which was later made into a movie.)[85]

Another example of using the things you read to enhance your talks and lessons is from L. Tom Perry of the Quorum of the Twelve, who talked about the funnies in the newspaper once in a talk titled "Making the Right Decisions." He shared an excerpt from the "Peanuts" comic strip, which showed the character Lucy walking up to Linus, who's holding a snowball. Elder Perry said:

She surveys the situation and makes this comment to Linus: "Life is full of choices. You may choose, if you wish, to throw that snow ball at me. You also may choose, if you wish, not to throw that snowball at me. Now if you choose to throw that snowball at me, I will pound you right into the ground! If you choose not to throw that snowball at me, your head will be spared."

Then Linus, throwing the snowball away with a disgusted look on his face, said, "Life is full of choices, but I never get any."[86]

FINDING STORIES ISN'T A PERSONALITY TRAIT, IT'S A DISCIPLINE

One of the best storytellers I know is my friend Blair M. Kent, who's a stake president in Highland, Utah, and the chief executive officer of Intermountain Medical Center, Utah's largest hospital. He's a skilled and prolific storyteller; in fact he sends an email every week to the hospital's 5,000 employees, titled "The Story of the Week," that includes an experience he's had and the lesson it taught him. Here's an example:

I went to lunch at a Kentucky Fried Chicken restaurant some years ago. I walked up to the counter and placed my order and the cashier was especially attentive, maybe even a little nervous. I thought: *Maybe she's new.*

I pulled out my wallet and the cashier said: *Oh, no, that's taken care of.* That seemed odd, but I thought maybe I was the millionth customer or something. The woman told me to take a seat and they'd bring my meal out to me, so I sat down, and in just a minute or two — faster than I expected — another KFC team member brought out my meal.

It was on a porcelain plate, and the person set out real silverware to go with it. I thought: *Wow! Note to self: Come here more often!*

I dug into my chicken and mashed potatoes, and a couple of minutes later, someone else came out and said: *Do you need anything else?* The way things were going, I wondered if I should ask for a pony. Five minutes after that someone else came out and said: Is everything *okay?* I said: *Okay? Man, it's finger-lickin' great. Real china, real silverware, and it's* free. *I'm good!*

And then someone else came out with a clipboard and started asking more questions: *How's the appearance of the store? How's the cleanliness? How's the temperature of your food?*

Then the questions got more specific, and the person with the clipboard called me something I've never been called before, even at work or on the freeway: *Mr. Johnson.* At that point a light started to come on — and I hustled to finish my lunch before they figured things out.

They thought I was a regional executive from KFC who was there to inspect their restaurant. My clothes set me up: I was wearing blue pants, a plaid shirt with beige and red stripes, and a red tie — the exact team colors of KFC. I fessed up and told them I wasn't Mr. Johnson, and we all laughed about it. I offered to pay for my meal, and they said, no, it's on us, and I looked at my shirt and tie and said: *Yes, and some of it's on me.*

I've never forgotten how good they treated me or how special I felt — and as I think about that story, I've thought: In our lives, and especially when we're at work, do we treat people differently based on their appearance or their status? Are we more polite to a manager than we are to a colleague? Are doctors more patient with another doc than they are with a nurse? If a patient appears to be destitute or even homeless, do we treat them differently than we would if we thought they were some kind of VIP?

The truth is, everyone's a VIP. Our value of mutual respect doesn't have any asterisks or exceptions. I'm proud to say I've seen that consistent level of respect everywhere I've gone in our hospital, including places where people didn't know I'm the administrator. That's made me feel very good — as good as I did during my visit to KFC.

And if you think that's the only thing I learned from my free lunch that day, you haven't seen my closet filled with outfits in the colors of Wendy's, McDonald's, Arby's, and Subway.

Just try to not run into me in front of Hot Dog on a Stick![87]

The leadership principle Blair practices is described like this in the *Harvard Business Review*: "Storytelling may seem like an old-fashioned tool today — and it is. That's exactly what makes it so powerful. Life happens in the narratives we tell one another. A story can go where quantitative analysis is denied admission: our hearts. Data can persuade people, but it doesn't inspire them to act; to do that, you need to wrap your vision in a story that fires the imagination and stirs the soul."[88]

At work and at church, Blair is always ready to share an experience that illustrates a principle or illuminates a problem, and many of his stories are hilarious. Here's one more short example, shared with his hospital team at the beginning of a new year:

I love potatoes. I love potatoes the way most people love chocolate. Baked, mashed, French fries, hash browns — yes, yes, yes, and yes. I believe one of the greatest inventions in the history of the world is the tater tot.

So a couple of years ago, Terri and I were at a German deli, looking at a really enticing display case, and I saw a bowl of potato-looking deliciousness labeled *schmaltz*, and I told the clerk: I've *never* said no to schmaltz — please pile some on my plate!

We sat down. I picked up my spoon. I scooped up a big bite of schmaltz and I found: Schmaltz is NOT potatoes. It's chicken fat. In fact it tastes exactly like you'd expect chicken fat to taste, only less chickeny. I immediately wondered: Where can I schpit it out?

It's a lesson I'll never forget, and it leads to this idea: Don't ever eat a spoonful of schmaltz — but don't be afraid to try new things, either.

Put some new in the new year by doing things you haven't done before. If you normally don't say hi to people in the elevator, try it. If you normally sit back in meetings while other people share their ideas, speak up. If you typically check your phone while you're walking down the hall, put it away and say hello to the people you walk past. Sit by someone new at lunch.

Be creative. After work, read a book by a new author. Take your kids someplace they've never been before. Check out a different news site on your phone.

And try a new restaurant. Just be careful about…well, you know.[89]

Blair's stories enhance his influence on both his employees and the members of his stake. I asked him once: Where do you *get* your stories? His answer: Remembering stories isn't a gift or a personality trait, it's a discipline — a skill he practices. For years he's kept notes in a series of notebooks, titled "Memories of a Lifetime," and when something happens that touches him, he jots down a line or two about it so he'll remember. He said, "It's gotten to the point where my wife makes fun of me. Something will happen and she can tell my mind is working, and she says, 'You're thinking of a talk.' She's on to my secret!"

He adds, "In terms of looking for spiritual experiences or stories that have happened to us, I think too often we look for miracles and big moments — we look for the Red Sea to part. Whatever lens we're looking through isn't focused on the moment. When you're paying attention, anything that happens to you can have messages or meaning. That's why I keep notes about the things that touch my heart or my mind. I think the discipline of observation is a gift we give ourselves that can bless everyone around us."[90]

A FEW THINGS TO WATCH OUT FOR WHEN YOU TELL STORIES

To avoid sharing personal experiences inappropriately, keep the following points in mind:

1. AVOID EMBARRASSING DETAILS. Although the best stories are taken directly from your life, details in those stories can be embarrassing and hurtful if a husband or wife or child is portrayed as a villain or a buffoon. Some stories that can increase your effectiveness as a speaker will decrease your effectiveness as a parent or a spouse. Avoid them. If an experience seems too personal or is potentially hurtful, don't tell it. Leave out unnecessary personal details. If necessary, get permission to tell a story from whoever the story involves. Be sensitive. Pray for the guidance of the Spirit.

2. DON'T EMBELLISH THE STORY. It can be tempting to make a story more dramatic or more emotional by altering some of the details of what happened. Don't do it. Be honest in your dealings. Telling the truth is always the right thing to do, and never more so than when you're teaching the gospel. Stretching the truth will diminish the Lord's Spirit, which is the source of any real impact your talk will have.

3. MAKE SURE YOUR STORY RELATES TO YOUR POINT. A story told merely to entertain can defeat the purpose of gospel teaching. Share your experiences strategically: Tie them to the scriptures and to the principles you're addressing. In a 1905 conference on teaching in the Church, President McKay said: "It is as necessary to study what not to put into your lesson as to know what to introduce into it. That teacher is the most successful who eliminates all non-essentials."[91]

4. AVOID MAKING YOURSELF THE HERO OF ALL OF YOUR STORIES. If you're always the good guy, you'll lose the credibility a personal story is supposed to help you gain. Remember: Self-deprecating stories usually work; self-aggrandizing stories usually don't.

5. BE SENSITIVE ABOUT THE PERSONAL SPIRITUAL EXPERIENCES YOU SHARE. "There are some things just too sacred to discuss," said Boyd K. Packer.[92] Elder Gene R. Cook adds: "Be cautious with spiritual experiences…There are some experiences that ought to be shared and some that ought not to be shared."[93] Follow the advice in Doctrine & Covenants 63:64: "Remember that that which cometh from above is sacred, and must be spoken with care, and by constraint of the Spirit."

6. WATCH OUT FOR REPETITION. It's easy to keep a catalogue of stories in your mind; when a certain topic comes up your mind will automatically default to a certain experience. But remember the old saying: "Stop me if you've heard this before" — and stop yourself from unnecessary repetition. Stretch your mind and your heart and expand your collection of personal experiences. Elder Cook says: "Don't just have some repertoire of experiences you traditionally tell (although it's good to have a repertoire), but constantly pray that the Lord will draw from you the one experience you really ought to share today."[94] A year or so after my mission, after I'd been teaching the elder's quorum for a while, I thought: *If all of my spiritual experiences are mission stories, then clearly it's time to lengthen my stride.*

Marjorie Hinckley illustrates the point. I love the humor Sister Hinckley often shared, including the gentle teasing she sometimes aimed at her husband, Gordon B. Hinckley. One example: Sister Hinckley's grandmother, Mary Goble, crossed the plains with the pioneers when she was just 13, and lost her mother, brother, sister — and, from frostbite, her toes — in the process. President Hinckley frequently recounted her hardships and faith. *Very* frequently, said Sister Hinckley. She wrote a letter to one of her children that said: "I am sitting in the Valley Music Hall, where Dad is the featured speaker at the regional fireside commemorating the handcart company. I can feel the Mary Goble story coming up fast."[95]

7. SHARE ENOUGH DETAILS TO BE MEMORABLE. Sharing too many details can drown your story in minutiae, but not sharing enough can make your story generic and forgettable. My friend Gary Pehrson, who served as president of the Connecticut Hartford Mission from 2008 to 2011, shows what I mean. This brief story strikes a perfect balance between being specific and memorable without slogging through the swamp of too many details. His experience is especially touching because it succinctly addresses a universal question among the saints: *How can you describe the influence of the Holy Ghost?* Gary said:

> While in the Boston Temple I had a not-too-often experience for me. As I was sitting there I wasn't really thinking about anything in particular. I was simply there enjoying the moment. My mind wasn't cluttered with anything. I realized as I sat there that I had an incredibly calm and peaceful feeling come over me. The feeling was so calming and peaceful that I felt completely at ease and comfortable with who I am, where I was at the time, and what we were doing here. This feeling was indeed a tender mercy from God. I wanted more of it, but soon the power of it departed. I still felt good, but now it became a memory I long to experience again. Of course, I recognize the feeling as the Holy Ghost, the Comforter.[96]

8. DON'T SHARE TOO MANY DETAILS. Keep your stories simple. Mozart is credited with a cacophonic example: "My great-grandfather used to say to his wife, my great-grandmother, who in turn told her daughter, my grandmother, who repeated it to her daughter, my mother, who used to remind her daughter, my own sister, that to talk well and eloquently was a very great art, but that an equally great one was to know the right moment to stop."[97]

A story about Albert Einstein's golf lesson provides another example. When some of Einstein's colleagues talked him into taking a lesson at a golf club near Princeton University, the great scientist was overwhelmed by the flood of directions his instructor gave him. Frustrated, the professor threw four golf balls in the air and told the golf pro to catch them — then watched all four fall to the ground. Einstein said, in his commanding German accent: "Young man, when I throw you one ball you catch it. However, when I throw you four balls, you catch nothing! So when you teach, make only one point at a time!"[98]

Same thing when you tell stories. Keep it simple.

A FINAL THOUGHT ON USING EXAMPLES

When you use examples in your talks and lessons, you're following the example of the leaders of the Church, who share personal stories to illustrate the lessons and principles they share; you're following the example of Nephi and Paul and Alma, who filled the scriptures with personal experiences; and you're following the Lord's example in telling stories and sharing parables.

Telling stories can be especially meaningful at home. In May 2020, early in the COVID-19 pandemic, when a formal church service hadn't been held for two months, my wife and I came to a powerful question one day in a "Come, Follow Me" discussion. The question asked: What places have special meaning to you because of the spiritual experiences you had there?[99] Laurie's answer was: "My mom's room on the day my dad died."

Her mom that day was in the advanced stages of Alzheimer's disease; she lived in the memory care unit of an assisted living center, and her dad was in a hospital room across town. Laurie was sitting with her mom when she got a text saying her dad was almost gone; she should hurry to the hospital so she could be with him as he slipped away. But she heard her dad's voice tell her: "Stay with mom. Laurie, promise me you'll take care of mom. I don't want her to be alone." Two minutes later, across the city, her dad died.

When Laurie answered that question about a place where she'd had a spiritual experience, we thought about her mom's room in the senior center. It was messy. It smelled. It was often an unhappy place. But it was a sacred grove to Laurie because of the experience she had there.

As you discuss the gospel at home or at church, you'll see the power a story can deliver. And you'll be following the advice — and the example — of David O. McKay. "Gather in experiences, and then illustrate each point," he said in a church-wide conference on teaching in 1905. "That is a lesson to every teacher."[100]

President McKay followed his own advice. In a 1912 conference talk, he shared this personal story:

> I remember lying in bed one night, trembling with fear. As a child I was naturally, or unnaturally, afraid of the darkness, and would frequently lie wondering about burglars, "bug-a-boos," and unseen influences. So I lay this night completely unnerved, but I had been taught that God would answer prayer. Summoning strength, I arose from the bed, knelt down in the darkness, and prayed to God to remove that feeling of fear — and I heard as plainly as you hear my voice this afternoon, "Don't be afraid; nothing will hurt you."
>
> Oh, yes, some may say: "Simply the imagination." Say what you will, I know that to my soul came the sweet peace of a child's prayer answered."[101]

As you listen to talks and lessons — and as you deliver them — you'll see the wisdom of President McKay's advice. And you'll see the truth of this reference from the *Church News*: "The gospel of Jesus Christ is, in large measure, a gospel of stories — stories that illustrate and illuminate, stories that inspire and encourage, stories that build faith and foster assurance, stories that reprove and admonish on occasion."[102]

CLARIFYING QUESTIONS: USE EXAMPLES

Share your answers and see what others have posted at BetterTalksLDS.com.

1. What stories about your parents or grandparents have helped shape your memories of them?

2. What stories influence how you view your workplace?

3. How have you been impacted by a story someone shared in a talk?

4. What stories do you recall hearing when you were young, and what did you learn from them?

5. Why do you think personal stories are credible and interesting?

6. What stories stand out to you from the most recent talks you've heard?

7. What's your favorite parable, and what lesson does it teach?

8. What would help you come up with a personal story to share in your next talk or lesson?

9. What stories from the scriptures are most meaningful to you?

EMPHASIZE APPLICATION

The best example of what it means to emphasize application may be from James the Apostle. "If any man lack wisdom," he wrote, "let him ask of God."

That's as application-oriented as any lesson ever taught. You read it, and you go away with a very definitive idea about what you should do. Bruce R. McConkie said: "This single verse of scripture has had a greater impact and a more far-reaching effect upon mankind than any other single sentence ever recorded by any prophet in any age."[103]

Look at its impact. One of James's students, the young Prophet Joseph, said: "Never did any passage of scripture come with more power to the heart of man than this did at this time to mine. It seemed to enter with great force into every feeling of my heart."

He added: "I reflected on it again and again." And then he applied it: "At length I came to the conclusion that I must either remain in darkness and confusion, or else I must do as James directs, that is, ask of God. I at length came to the determination to 'ask of God,' concluding that if he gave wisdom to them that lacked wisdom, and would give liberally, and not upbraid, I might venture."[104] That's what application means — it happens when the people who hear our talks and lessons remember the principles we've talked about and put them to work in their lives. Application is action; the dictionary defines it *as the act of putting something into operation.*

Here's a personal example. When I was 11, I got a paper route, delivering an afternoon paper. Every day after school I rode my bike to a paper stop where a delivery truck would drop off bundles of papers for three or four paper carriers. As soon as the truck came, we'd fold the papers, pack them into canvas bags, drape the bags over our handlebars, and pedal away to deliver them.

And every day, while we waited for the paper truck to arrive, we'd sit on the lawn and talk about things pre-teen boys talked about. One of the other paperboys and I stuck to a consistent conversational theme — trading insults. He provided lots of material to cover, because I didn't like him. I didn't like the way he looked or the way he acted, and every day while we waited for our papers, I pointed out his failings. He wore glasses, for one thing, and that made him look like a weirdo. I had strong evidence, since *I* wore glasses, too, and mine made *me* look like a weirdo. He had a bad haircut — not at all like the haircuts of the Beatles, who set the standard for cool haircuts at that time, which my parents failed to understand, which is why I had a haircut like his, too.

Roger and I were a lot alike, in other words. Maybe that's why we didn't like each other. Trading insults every day was our paper route tradition; it was what we did before the truck came. We weren't bullies and we weren't bad kids. We were just dumb; we both thought that putting the other boy down built us up.

Around that time I turned 12. My dad ordained me to the priesthood and I started going to my deacons quorum every Sunday, which felt dramatically more grown-up than Primary. The culture was different. Our quorum had a good adviser; he taught good lessons — and he asked us questions and addressed us like we knew something, instead of like kids. As a result, we paid attention. We didn't squirm or mess around in class. I don't remember many specific lessons, but our adviser told a lot of scripture stories, and he illustrated his lessons with examples from his work in the chemistry department at the University of Utah, where he was a graduate student. Being in the deacons quorum was like being a grown-up, in a religious sense. I wasn't a kid anymore.

As I went to our quorum meetings on Sunday, then rode to the paper stop during the week to trade insults with Roger, pretty soon an idea occurred to me: I ought to treat Roger better than I was treating him. I shouldn't try to put him down. So I determined to do better. I *applied* what I was learning in my quorum on Sunday. One afternoon I rode to the paper stop, got off my bike to wait for the truck, and sat by Roger, who started in with whatever came to mind: *Man, Rich, where'd you get that shirt? It's hideous! Did your maaaaaaaahm buy it for you?* (And note: That would have been easy to defend. *All* moms bought *all* clothes back then. How else could you get them? My mom bought mine at the start of each school year and Roger's mom bought his. The quality of that insult was insulting.)

But I was no longer a member of the insult club. I said something like: *Well, Roger, I'm sorry my shirt has offended you. I'll try to choose something better tomorrow.* He tried another attack, but I responded with a white flag to that one, too. Roger: *Your bike is a piece of junk. Look at it! Haven't you ever heard of oil?* Me: *Yes, it's not nearly as nice as your bike.*

He didn't know how to respond. He must have thought I'd bumped my head and forgotten who I was. But when the truck came and dropped off our papers, we folded them in peaceful silence, packed up, and rode away to do our routes. The next day, same thing: Roger fired a couple of insult missiles, and I didn't return fire. I had decided that a deacon and a priesthood-holder ought to talk to people — including Roger, who was probably also a deacon — more respectfully than I'd been talking to him. My goal was to follow Paul's example: *When I was a child, I spoke as a child, but when I became a man, I stopped calling people childish names.* Roger was perplexed, and possibly disappointed. Waiting for the papers was probably a little more boring in our post-insult world. But I'd made my decision to start living the principles I was learning, even if Roger had to pay the price.

I've wondered since then: What made me change my behavior? I don't remember a specific lesson in the deacon's quorum on uplifting language or treating people with respect. All I remember is that I felt I needed to improve my behavior and act the way deacons were supposed to act.

WHAT DOES IT MEAN TO EMPHASIZE APPLICATION?

A couple of years after my newspaper delivery career ended, I posted this quote from the British scientist T.H. Huxley on a corkboard in my room: "The great end of life is not knowledge, but action." Elder Dieter F. Uchtdorf reinforced that thought in a 2012 conference address: "It is in the application of doctrine that the purifying flame of the gospel grows and the power of the priesthood ignites our souls. Thomas Edison, the man who bathed the world in glowing electric light, said 'the value of an idea lies in the using of it.'"[105]

The "Come, Follow Me" manual, a powerful resource that's helping gospel learning be home-centered and Church-supported, says: "Learning is not complete until we follow the Savior by living what he taught."[106] The introduction to the manual says: "Scripture study should not only inspire us — it should lead us to change the way we live...After reading a scripture passage, ask family members to share ways the passage applies to their lives."[107]

Lancelot Andrewes, an Anglican bishop who helped translate the Bible in the 1500s and early 1600s, said: "The only true praise of a sermon is some evil left abandoned, or some good done, upon the hearing of it."[108] And the Lord says in D&C 43:8: "And now, behold, I give unto you a commandment, that when ye are assembled together ye shall instruct and edify each other, that ye may know how to act and direct my church, how to act upon the points of my law and commandments, which I have given."

By emphasizing application, we encourage appropriate action. President Dallin H. Oaks shared this advice in a powerful conference address titled "Gospel Teaching" in October 1999:

> A gospel teacher is concerned with the results of his or her teaching, and such a teacher will measure the success of teaching and testifying by its impact on the lives of the learners. A gospel teacher will never be satisfied with just delivering a message or preaching a sermon. A superior gospel teacher wants to assist in the Lord's work to bring eternal life to His children.[109]

WHY EMPHASIZING APPLICATION IS IMPORTANT

Here's an example of how talks or lessons can influence our lives: In about 1987, I cut down a dead tree in the middle of our backyard, then started to dig out the stump. I was working on the stump on a Saturday afternoon, using a shovel and an ax, and when I needed a break I laid on the grass to stretch my sore back. Our daughter Emily, who was three, came into the backyard carrying a Kleenex — she'd had a runny nose. She walked over to check out what I was doing, sat down and put her bare feet into the hole I'd dug around the stump, then reached in and picked something up. I sat up to see what she was holding.

She'd pulled a worm out of the soft dirt, and she was rubbing it with her Kleenex. "Em, what are you doing with that worm?" I said. She said, with an answer that's now legendary in our family: "Me wiping him's nose."

I wondered: Where did Emily learn that kind of kindness? No one told her how to treat that worm. I didn't even notice if it looked sick. But she was an enthusiastic Sunbeam, an active participant in our home evenings and family prayers, and an inherently empathetic little girl, and she decided on her own how to apply the principles she'd been learning.

That echoes the Prophet Joseph's response when a member of the Illinois legislature asked how he encouraged the faithfulness of the early Saints so effectively and how he maintained order among so many followers. "I teach them correct principles, and they govern themselves," he said.[110] As teachers in the kingdom, that's our job, too.

David O. McKay expressed the principle of emphasizing application like this: "Feeling anything without acting does not amount to much." In a church-wide Sunday School conference in 1907, he talked about how a teacher could share the story of the Lord driving the moneychangers out of the temple. "Present that lesson and make the child feel that the house of the Lord is a house of order," he said. But then he asked a question: What if later that day you saw one of your students putting his hat on the sacrament table? "Have you taught the child that lesson?" he asked. "No — the teacher may have presented the lesson in a noble way and an interesting way, but she failed to open the avenues of the question."[111] Those avenues lead to applying the lessons you teach. President McKay said:

It is not enough to know what is good, we must do good. A child may be taught in the Sunday School obedience to his parents, and go home and say, "I won't do it."…There is something lacking in his teaching. The teacher failed to apply the lesson aim. She failed to show the child how he could introduce the truth into his life — into his life *today*.[112]

An account of President McKay's teachings almost 60 years later, printed in *The Instructor* (which was an official church publication from 1930 to 1970), said: "Teachers soon felt that unless every pupil left the class with a burning desire to do something as a direct result of Sunday's lesson, they had failed in their presentation of the subject. The admonition, 'Be ye doers of the word, and not hearers only' (James 1:22) is certainly a measure of effective…teaching."[113]

One addendum from President Oaks' 1999 address on gospel teaching: "Teachers who are commanded to teach 'the principles of [the] gospel' and 'the doctrine of the kingdom' (D&C 88:77) should generally forgo teaching specific rules or applications. For example, they would not teach any rules for determining what is a full tithing, and they would not provide a list of dos and don'ts for keeping the Sabbath day holy." In other words, be careful about "looking beyond the mark," as Jacob 4:14 advises, or injecting your opinions or enthusiasms into gospel doctrines, and be careful about trampling on anyone's free agency.

But do encourage people to act. Follow President McKay's advice: Every talk and lesson you give should encourage people to apply — on their own, according to their own conscience — the gospel principles you're addressing. Again, remember Elder Oaks' counsel: "A gospel teacher is concerned with the results of his or her teaching, and such a teacher will measure the success of teaching and testifying by its impact on the lives of the learners. A gospel teacher will never be satisfied with just delivering a message or preaching a sermon."

The "Come, Follow Me" manual is packed with questions that emphasize how to apply the gospel principles we learn in our studies. As the manual spotlights scriptures on different topics, it asks application-oriented questions like this:

- Examine your schedule — is there something "needful" that needs more of your attention?[114]

- How does hatred cause us to walk in darkness and stumble? How does loving each other bring light and life in our lives?

- Is your family running faster than you have strength?

- What are some specific things we can do to help fill the earth with "the knowledge of the Lord"?

WE'RE ASKED TO BE DOERS OF THE WORD
AND NOT HEARERS ONLY

Elder Gene R. Cook, in *Teaching By The Spirit*, reiterates James' action-oriented advice: He says the Lord's Spirit doesn't tell us things on an FYI basis. "I believe that when the Holy Ghost teaches us something, it's normally not just for our information," he says. "The Spirit doesn't seem to spend a lot of time on purely academic issues. Instead, the Lord generally tells us things to help us to repent and do better in our lives. We need to take the same approach in our teaching. One element of teaching by the Spirit is to apply the truths to the individuals in the class."[118]

Here's a job-related example. One of my friends is Dr. Mark Ott, who served as the medical director of the hospital where I spent my career; he was in charge of making sure 1,800 physicians and the staff members who supported them followed the hospital's policies and advanced its standards. Mark, who is a nationally prominent cancer surgeon who's served as a bishop twice — once in Belmont, Massachusetts, and once in Salt Lake City — told me this story:

A few months ago I was completing a complex surgery on a patient who had cancer. The procedure had gone well, but at the end of the operation I noticed the scrub tech and circulating nurse talking in subdued tones to each other. They seemed a little anxious about something, but clearly they were trying to figure it out without bothering me. Finally, as I was suturing the patient's abdomen closed, I looked over to them and said: "Is something wrong?" Neither one answered at first; they just looked at each other. Then the scrub tech said: "Our counts are off by one sponge." It was clear to me that they assumed they'd made an error in their counting.

I stopped what I was doing, made another careful inspection of the entire abdomen, and found the sponge I'd missed when I'd checked it prior to closure. I took it out, we closed the abdominal incision, and the case ended well.

But one thing bothered me: *Why did the scrub tech and nurse hesitate?* They'd noticed a problem I didn't notice — yet they were hesitant to speak up.

I scheduled a meeting with all of our general surgery team scrub techs and nurses. I started the meeting by saying: "Surgery is an intense experience for all of us. Sometimes a patient's life hangs in the balance, and there's a lot of pressure on us to perform *perfectly*. In that environment, I know that I, like many surgeons, can be intimidating — and I'm sometimes not as patient and respectful as I should be. I want things to go perfectly in every operation, but we can't achieve perfection if surgeons act like autocrats and create an environment where they can't be questioned."

I confessed to our talented team: "I know I've acted like that in the past and I never want to be that way again. I'm sorry for that behavior. It's incredibly stressful when we're having a difficult operation, when everyone's doing their best to care for the patient, and I allow myself to get frustrated because something wasn't done the way I wanted it." I've always rationalized that my behavior was in the best interests of my patients — but I was wrong, because acting like a tyrant squelches the collaboration that helps make a surgery or any kind of healthcare procedure more successful.

In his speech in the meeting, Mark didn't seek to exercise control or dominion or compulsion; instead, he followed the Lord's advice in D&C 121 and used persuasion, long-suffering, gentleness and meekness, love unfeigned, kindness, and pure knowledge. He said:

I asked the scrub techs and nurses for their forgiveness. I told them: "I always need you to speak up when you have a concern. Every person's voice needs to be heard in such a critical team endeavor. As a surgeon, I need that collaboration with all the members of the OR team. I can't be a leader in the OR or in our hospital system if you feel like you can't talk with me. I'm committing to change."

When I finished, I had tears in my eyes — and there was absolute silence in the room. I don't think the 40 members of our team had ever had a surgeon do or say anything like that in a staff meeting.

Then to my relief, they began to clap. I could feel their outpouring of understanding, support, and forgiveness. It was a tremendous experience. As I left the meeting I thought: This is one of the best days of my life. I'm being given a new chance by these wonderful people to become a better surgeon and a better person.

Mark asked for greater teamwork not only with his words, but with his demeanor. His focus was on action: *Please help me. Speak up. Strengthen our team.* He demonstrated an emphasis on application that's part of all high-impact teaching.[119]

ADVICE FROM CHURCH LEADERS
ABOUT EMPHASIZING APPLICATION

Merlin R. Lybbert of the Seventy shared a great story about the need to apply gospel principles in a 1990 conference address. He said: "An enterprising turkey gathered the flock together and, following instructions and demonstrations, taught them how to fly. All afternoon they enjoyed soaring and flying and the thrill of seeing new vistas. After the meeting, all of the turkeys walked home." Elder Lybbert then added: "It is not our understanding of the principles of the gospel that brings the blessings of heaven, but the living of them."[120]

Related instructions from other church leaders, past and present, reiterate the point:

- Gordon B. Hinckley: "Eternal life will come only as men and women are taught with such effectiveness that they change and discipline their lives."[121]

- Dallin H. Oaks: "The gospel challenges us to be 'converted,' which requires us to *do* and to *become*. If any of us relies solely upon our knowledge and testimony of the gospel, we are in the same position as the blessed but still unfinished apostles whom Jesus challenged to be 'converted.'"[122]

- Bonnie D. Parkin, general president of the Relief Society: "To know is to do!"[123]

- Benjamin M. Z. Tai of the Seventy: "By consistently applying the doctrine of Christ in our lives, we will overcome inertia that impedes change and fear that foils action."[124]

- Thomas S. Monson: "The goal of gospel teaching today, as emphasized in the teacher development program, is not to 'pour information' into the minds of class members. It is not to show how much the teacher knows, nor is it merely to increase knowledge about the Church. The basic goal of teaching in the Church is to help bring about worthwhile changes in the lives of boys and girls, men and women. The aim is to inspire the individual to think about, feel about, and then do something about living gospel principles."[125]

- Russell T. Osguthorpe, general president of the Sunday School: "Conversion is the goal of all gospel learning and teaching."[126]

- Marion G. Romney of the First Presidency: "While the Lord will magnify us in both subtle and dramatic ways, he can only guide our footsteps when we move our feet. Ultimately, our own actions determine our blessings or lack of them."[127]

- James H. Bekker, an Area Seventy: "The Lord can't steer a parked car."[128]

Alma is an example of a church leader who effectively encouraged people to apply gospel principles — as demonstrated by the life of Alma the Younger, his son. The younger Alma describes his response to a visit from an angel in Alma 36, and in the midst of three days of being "racked with torment, while I was harrowed up by the memory of my many sins," he says: "I remembered also to have heard my father prophecy unto the people concerning the coming of one Jesus Christ, a Son of God, to atone for the sins of the world." The fact that he remembered his father's words bespeaks the power of effective teaching, but the takeaway from Alma the Younger's experience was demonstrated by his effort to act on what his father said, which he recounts like this:

Now, as my mind caught hold upon this thought, I cried within my heart: O Jesus, thou Son of God, have mercy on me, who am in the gall of bitterness, and am encircled about by the everlasting chains of death. And now, behold, when I thought this, I could remember my pains no more; yea, I was harrowed up by the memory of my sins no more. And oh, what joy, and what marvelous light I did behold; yea, my soul was filled with joy as exceeding as was my pain! Yea, I say unto you, my son, that there could be nothing so exquisite and so bitter as were my pains. Yea, and again I say unto you, my son, that on the other hand, there can be nothing so exquisite and sweet as was my joy.[129]

That's a *perfect* example of the power that ensues when we apply the gospel lessons we hear.

EIGHT WAYS TO EMPHASIZE APPLICATION IN YOUR TALKS AND LESSONS

Once you've prepared your lesson — once you've chosen an objective and thought of examples to illustrate it — you're not done until you've answered the question: *What do I want people to DO because they heard my lesson or my talk?* King Benjamin made that point toward the end of his landmark address when he told his people: "If you believe all these things, see that ye do them" (Mosiah 4:10). John the Beloved taught the same principle: "He that doeth truth cometh to the light" (John 3:21).

Here are eight suggestions to help you follow the advice of President McKay — and King Benjamin, John, and every leader of the Church, from the beginning of the world to today — to emphasize action whenever you speak or teach:

1. FOCUS ON THE GOAL OF ACTION AS YOU PREPARE YOUR TALK OR LESSON.
Stephen Covey phrases that advice like this: Begin with the end in mind. He said: "How different our lives are when we really know what is deeply important to us, and, keeping that picture in mind, we manage ourselves each day to be and to do what really matters most. If the ladder is not leaning against the right wall, every step we take will get us to the wrong place faster. We may be very busy, we may be very efficient, but we will also be truly *effective* only when we begin with the end in mind."[130]

Plant the flag of application in your mind as you sit down to prepare your notes. President McKay's advice to emphasize application helped me learn this habit when I taught gospel doctrine: Before I started to prepare a lesson, I asked myself (and the Lord) these questions: What do the members of the class *need this week?* When they leave our class, what should they be prepared to do? I found: When you ask the Lord in advance to help you focus on applying your message, the thoughts you receive in response will shape what you say.

2. ASK QUESTIONS — RHETORICALLY OR PRACTICALLY. As part of your talks and lessons, ask your listeners: So what can we do to implement what we're learning here? What can you do to live the principles I'm talking about? My friend Rich Cannon, who's the patriarch of my stake, talked about his calling at a fireside in the spring of 2016, and he asked this question: If you were called to be a patriarch, and you needed constant access to the Lord's spirit, what in your life would you have to give up? (And he added, only partly in jest, that he had to give up Fox News.) I've talked about that question with many of the people who heard Rich's talk; the answers have been profound and influential.

I love what Rosemary M. Wixom, former general president of the Primary, said in a 2015 conference address: "Now it is time to take that beloved phrase 'I am a child of God' and add the words 'Therefore, what?'" Those two words — "Therefore, what?" — would be a great addendum to every scripture that's quoted in every talk in the Church.

Sister Wixom added: "We might even ask questions such as these: 'What will I do to live my life as a child of God?' 'How can I develop the divine nature that is within me?'"[131]

3. EMPHASIZE APPLICATION *EARLY* IN YOUR TALKS AND LESSONS. Encouraging your listeners to apply your message may naturally fit in at the end of your remarks, but because you often run out of time by the time your talk or lesson is over, don't be shy about addressing it earlier. Remember: The things we say on Sunday should always lead to practical takeaways that enhance our lives once Monday arrives. "We talk glibly about eternal progress," said Neal A. Maxwell in a talk at BYU. "Yet that idea really must be broken down into day-by-by improvement."[132]

4. SHARE CHALLENGES AND INVITATIONS. Ever since Moroni included his challenge at the end of the Book of Mormon, speakers in every meeting in the Church have challenged us to apply the principles of the gospel. Some examples from leaders of the Church:

- Michael John U. Teh of the Seventy: "I challenge you to commit to reading the scriptures daily. Do not go to bed tonight until you have read."[133]

- Bonnie L. Oscarson, general president of the Young Women: "I am grateful to be a woman in these latter days. We have opportunities and possibilities which no other generation of women has had in the world. Let us help build the kingdom of God by standing up boldly and being defenders of marriage, parenthood, and the home. The Lord needs us to be brave, steadfast, and immovable warriors who will defend His plan and teach the upcoming generations His truths."[134]

- James O. Mason, MD, commissioner of the Health Services Corporation of the Church: "I challenge you to prepare for missionary calls, not only to go out and preach the gospel of Jesus Christ at home and abroad, but to go forth in love and brotherhood, using your professional and vocational skills to reach out and lift up."[135]

- Elaine S. Dalton, general president of the Young Women: "Young women, generations are depending on the choices you make, your purity, and your worthy lives. Be not moved. You have a great destiny before you. This is your moment! I truly believe that one virtuous young woman, led by the Spirit, can change the world!"[136]

- Quentin L. Cook of the Quorum of the Twelve: "I challenge all of us to work with people of other faiths to improve the moral fabric of our communities, nations, and world and to protect religious freedom."[137]

When I was very young I heard about a bishop who invited a few members of his ward to spend two weeks living on their food storage — and avoid going to the grocery store — then report what happened in sacrament meeting. I remember thinking: Wow, I didn't know sacrament meeting talks were allowed to be so *interesting*. Years later when I was a bishop, our ward tried some similar application-oriented experiments: Several of our members reported what happened after they spent two weeks reading the scriptures every day and two weeks not reading. Another set of speakers skipped TV for a week and reported on the spiritual and practical blessings they harvested.

I saw an internet meme that said: "The difference between who you are and who you want to be is what you do." That's the point of sharing a challenge.

5. TALK ABOUT HOW YOU'VE APPLIED THE LESSONS YOU LEARNED.

Your experiences will motivate your listeners to think about what they can do to live the principles you talk about. That's how people think. Include application in your stories (because people remember stories). One of my favorite stories about my dad, Karl E. Nash, illustrates the principle of agency — and provides an excellent example of using consequences to raise a child: When dad was a teenager, he got up one Sunday morning and told his mom he wasn't going to church. That surely must have bothered his mom, who was raising four kids as a widowed mother, but she didn't voice any agitation. She just said: "Well, okay. Just make sure you have dinner ready when we get home." Dad said later: After that he attended his meetings *every* Sunday.

Another example: In general conference in October 1972, Bruce R. McConkie gave his first address as a newly-called apostle. He included this thought in his remarks: "I know there is revelation in the Church because I have received revelation. I know God speaks in this day because he has spoken to me."[138] That comment struck me with electrical force — and I grafted that segment of Elder McConkie's testimony into my testimony: I know God speaks to his prophets because he's spoken to me. I know the leaders of the Church are inspired because I've been inspired in my callings.

6. LIKEN THE SCRIPTURES UNTO YOURSELF (AND UNTO YOUR LISTENERS).

Following Nephi's advice to liken the scriptures unto yourself will help people know how to apply the doctrines you discuss. Again, my dad provides an example. When my younger brother, Scott, was 14 or 15, he did something that got him in trouble at home. Dad levied an appropriate punishment, then he implemented what the Lord advised in D&C 121: 41: After reproving Scott with sharpness, he showed an increase of love. Dad took him to the empty parking lot of the University of Utah football stadium, which was near our home, and let Scott — who was too young to hold a driver's license — spend a happy hour driving the car. Years later at my dad's funeral, Scott said he didn't remember what he did wrong, but he does remember the increase in love: "Whatever I did, I probably wanted to do it again so I could get another punishment like that. But when I think about it, dad's love and faithfulness, as promised in Section 121, came through loud and clear. Dad was a gentle, wise, loving father."

When Jeffrey R. Holland was serving as the Church's commissioner of education, he said: "Immerse yourself in the scriptures. You will find your own experiences described there. You will find spirit and strength there. You will find solutions and counsel. Nephi says, 'The words of Christ will tell you all things what you should do' (2 Nephi 32:3)."[139]

It's tempting to share scripture stories when you talk. But that's not likening the scriptures; that's quoting or paraphrasing them. Telling scripture stories can be effective. But telling your own stories, then likening what you experienced to the principles the scriptures teach, can be powerful. Allen D. Haynie of the Seventy shared a vivid illustration — which includes a profound example of how to *apply* a scriptural principle — in an October 2015 general conference address:

When I was nine years old, my white-haired, four-foot-eleven-inch maternal grandmother came to spend a few weeks with us at our home. One afternoon while she was there, my two older brothers and I decided to dig a hole in a field across the street from our house. I don't know why we did it; sometimes boys dig holes. We got a little dirty but nothing that would get us into too much trouble. Other boys in the neighborhood saw just how exciting it was to dig a hole and started to help. Then we all got dirtier together. The ground was hard, so we dragged a garden hose over and put a little water in the bottom of the hole to soften up the ground. We got some mud on us as we dug, but the hole did get deeper.

Someone in our group decided we should turn our hole into a swimming pool, so we filled it up with water. Being the youngest and wanting to fit in, I was persuaded to jump in and try it out. Now I was really dirty. I didn't start out planning to be covered in mud, but that's where I ended up.

When it started to get cold, I crossed the street, intending to walk into my house. My grandmother met me at the front door and refused to let me in. She told me that if she let me in, I would track mud into the house that she had just cleaned. So I did what any nine-year-old would do under the circumstances and ran to the back door, but she was quicker than I thought. I got mad, stomped my feet, and demanded to come into the house, but the door remained closed.

I was wet, muddy, cold, and, in my childhood imagination, thought I might die in my own backyard. Finally, I asked her what I had to do to come into the house. Before I knew it, I found myself standing in the backyard while my grandmother sprayed me off with a hose. After what seemed like an eternity, my grandmother pronounced me clean and let me come into the house. It was warm in the house, and I was able to put on dry, clean clothes.

With that real-life parable of sorts in mind, please consider the following words of Jesus Christ: "And no unclean thing can enter into his kingdom; therefore nothing entereth into his rest save it be those who have washed their garments in my blood, because of their faith, and the repentance of all their sins, and their faithfulness unto the end."

Elder Haynie applied that scripture — from 3 Nephi 27:19 — like this:

Standing outside of my house being sprayed off by my grandmother was unpleasant and uncomfortable. Being denied the opportunity to return and be with our Father in Heaven because we chose to remain in or dirtied by a mud hole of sin would be eternally tragic. We should not deceive ourselves about what it takes to return and remain in the presence of our Father in Heaven. We have to be clean.[140]

7. TALK ABOUT THE BLESSINGS OF LIVING THE PRINCIPLE YOU'RE ADDRESSING. Share examples of how the Lord blesses those who live the gospel. John 13:17 says: "If ye know these things, happy are ye if ye do them." Talk about that happiness and the other blessings that follow obedience to the gospel. The popular hymn phrases the idea like this: "Count your blessings, name them one by one; count your many blessings, see what God hath done." [141] Thomas S. Monson said: "Ours is the task to be fitting examples. We are strengthened by the truth that the greatest force in the world today is the power of God as it works through man."[142]

Sales people use this phrase to express the concept: Sell the benefits, not the features. If you're trying to sell a car, don't say it has a new kind of forced-air, energy-efficient air conditioning system. Instead, say: This car will keep you and your entire family unbelievably comfortable — including everyone in front and in back — in the summer when you're taking everyone to Disney World.

In more soaring terms, Neal Maxwell said, "The gospel, in fact, gives us glimpses of the far horizon, revealing a glow from the lights of the City of God."

Take a moment to describe that glow.[143]

8. BE SPECIFIC. Sometimes it's wise to be direct when you share advice about how people can apply the principles you discuss. A famous story told about Calvin Coolidge shows what happens when you're vague. The president, who was known as "Silent Cal" because he was so stingy with words, left the White House to go to church one Sunday morning, and when he returned, his wife asked what the preacher had talked about. "Sin," said Coolidge. "And what did he say about sin?" said Mrs. Coolidge. The president responded: "He was against it."[144]

Dieter F. Uchtdorf was much more specific in an April 2012 general conference address. He said, "This topic of judging others could actually be taught in a two-word sermon. When it comes to hating, gossiping, ignoring, ridiculing, holding grudges, or wanting to cause harm, please apply the following: Stop it!" *That's* specific advice.[145]

Likewise, one of my mission buddies, Charles Steinman, a powerfully effective missionary from New York who served with me in Southern California, tracted out a man who was belligerent and argumentative. The man mocked the message Elder Steinman and his companion were trying to deliver; he loudly and proudly recounted a detailed list of the commandments he'd broken and sins he'd committed: Immorality, drunkenness, blasphemy, irreverence, pride, lying, cheating, etc., etc. "What do you say to *that?*" said the man. "You're going to hell," said Elder Steinman. The man was speechless. He had no rebuttal to that brief — and very specific — response.

So be specific when you emphasize application. Don't trample on your listeners' agency — but don't leave them thinking: *I wonder what she meant when she said she was against sin?*

A FINAL THOUGHT ABOUT EMPHASIZING APPLICATION

My daughter Emily taught a surprise lesson about the plan of salvation to my mom, Rita Jones Nash, when Em was just three. Emily was playing with the magnetic letters on Grandma's refrigerator one morning, and after some random arranging, Grandma called out, "Look, Em, you spelled 'old'— o-l-d."

Little Em looked at the letters, then looked at my mom. "Grandma, you is old," she said.

My mom wasn't ruffled. "Yes, Emily, I am. I'm a grandma, and grandmas are old."

Em thought about her other grandmother. My wife's mom, who was friends with my mom, is 10 years younger than my mom — and Em had noticed. She said: "Grandma *Bonnie* isn't old."

I'm sure my mom loved hearing that. But she responded like a soldier. She said yes, Grandma Bonnie was much younger than she was.

Emily wasn't done. She said, "Grandma, soon you will die." At that point I think Mom would have been justified in taking all the magnets off the fridge and finding another game to play, but Mom responded well: She scooped Emily up into her arms, sat down with her on a kitchen chair, and said, "Yes, Emily, soon I'll die. But that will be a good thing. I'll go back to heaven, and I'll see my mom and dad and my brother and my sisters, and even though I'll miss you, I'll be really happy to be with them and with Heavenly Father again."

Emily and my mom were both teachers at heart — and I followed their examples. I think I've told the refrigerator magnet story in about half of the 35 or 40 funerals I've conducted or addressed. Often I'd end the story by saying: *Emily was right — all of us will die. None of us can escape it. But all of us can prepare for it by following the Lord, whose spirit whispers to our spirits that life continues after death. Jesus said: "I am the resurrection and the life; he that believeth in me, though he were dead, yet shall he live."* I've testified many times that the Lord will call our names, just as he called the name of Lazarus: "Lazarus, come forth." And as the scripture records: "He that was dead came forth."

Emphasizing application in our talks and lessons does more than help us be ready when we die. It helps us live the gospel every day. It helps us be doers of the word, not hearers only. Heber J. Grant, the seventh president of the Church, said in general conference in 1939: "Faith and knowledge without practice are of no value. All the knowledge in the world would not amount to anything unless we put that knowledge into actual practice. We are the architects and builders of our lives, and if we fail to put our knowledge into actual practice and do the duties that devolve upon us, we are making a failure of life."[146]

That's why emphasizing action is important. When we successfully fill our callings as speakers and teachers, we help the people who listen to us succeed in their callings as moms and dads, sons and daughters, brothers and sisters, and children of God.

CLARIFYING QUESTIONS: EMPHASIZE APPLICATION

Share your answers and see what others have posted at BetterTalksLDS.com.

1. When has applying a lesson or principle you learned in a talk made a difference in your life?

2. What examples of application can you think of in recent talks you've heard?

3. When have you heard a story that motivated you to live a gospel principle?

4. When has a speaker given you a direct challenge to apply a gospel principle in your life?

DELIVERING THE MESSAGE

Now that we've covered the three parts of David O. McKay's advice on how to give a talk, here's a suggestion for extra credit. If you write out your talk before you speak, print a copy, then stand at the podium and read it word for word, do this: *Read Doctrine & Covenants 100: 5-6.*

In that passage — and in similar passages in the scriptures — the Lord says, "Therefore, verily I say unto you, lift up your voices unto this people; speak the thoughts that I shall put into your hearts, and you shall not be confounded before men; *For it shall be given you in the very hour, yea, in the very moment, what ye shall say* (emphasis added)."

If you're a leader in the Church, if you've spoken often enough that you have some skill at it, if you're just interested in improving the way you speak, or if you want to strengthen your faith, here's why you should think seriously about speaking from notes instead of reading a prepared text next time you give a talk: When you're not bound word-for-word to your prepared text, the Lord's Spirit can tell you in the very moment what you should say. The Lord says in Matthew 10:20 why that advice is important: "For it is not ye that speak, but the Spirit of your Father which speaketh in you."

You may say: No way. I'm *terrified* of public speaking, and nothing would scare me as much as being in front of people without a written text, and I'd probably get all flustered and forget what I meant to say, and I might get emotional and cry and embarrass myself, plus I believe Jerry Seinfeld wasn't really joking when he said studies show people's top fear is public speaking, and death is second. Seinfeld added: "This means to the average person, if you go to a funeral, you're better off in the casket than doing the eulogy."[147]

You may also say: The Lord can inspire me just as easily on Saturday afternoon when I'm writing my talk as He can on Sunday morning when I'm delivering it.

The answer is: Yes, but Saturday afternoon isn't the very hour when you're speaking. Speaking from notes — and being free to choose your words in the moment you're saying them — enhances not only the Lord's ability to shape what you say, but it strengthens your emotional connection with your audience. Certainly there's a chance you'll forget what you meant to say, wander all over the place, and not only embarrass yourself, but bore the people in your ward or stake or branch and maybe even waste their time. *But that risk diminishes when you follow President McKay's advice* — when you:

1. Have an objective
2. Use examples
3. Emphasize application

Specifically, using examples — sharing your personal experiences — will make it easier for you to speak without a written script. You'll tell your stories from the podium in the same way you'd tell them to your friends or family. A miracle will happen then: You'll feel more comfortable. That will be followed by another miracle: The people you're addressing will be more engaged.

INSTEAD OF WRITING OUT YOUR TALK, LEAN ON THIS CRUTCH INSTEAD

My advice is to list President McKay's elements — your objective, the stories you want to tell, scriptures or quotes you feel impressed to use, and questions or points that will help your listeners apply what you're talking about — in an outline, or write them on a note card. That way you'll be organized; you'll have a crutch that will do what crutches do: Keep you from falling on your face. You'll be prepared, in a faithful way, and either you shall not fear, as D&C 38:30 promises — or, more likely, you'll fear in a manageable way.

The fear of public speaking is very real. I feel it every time I speak, and I don't know anyone who doesn't. But giving in to that fear by leaning on a written speech reduces the faith you can show, and grow, by giving the Lord an opportunity to direct your thoughts and words. The *perfection* that comes when you read your talk exactly as you wrote it, using only the words you typed into your word processor, can be replaced by *connection* — to the Lord's Spirit and to your audience — when you trust the Lord to give you the thoughts he'll put in your heart.

An article in the *New Era* on how to speak in sacrament meeting reiterated the wisdom of speaking from an outline. "Don't just read your talk with your head down," it said. The article advised:

It is often better to prepare a simple outline of what you are to speak on instead of writing the talk out word for word and reading it. Reading a talk may tie you down to say exactly what is written instead of being able to adapt as the Holy Ghost gives you "in the very moment, what ye shall say" (D&C 100:6).

President Gordon B. Hinckley taught, "We must ... speak out of [our] hearts rather than out of [our] books." By making your own experiences and testimony a vital part of your talk, you will be more likely to speak from your heart and affect those who hear your talk.[148]

KEY ADVANTAGES OF NOT WRITING OUT YOUR TALK: VULNERABILITY, HUMILITY, AND CONNECTION

One of the benefits you'll harvest is *vulnerability*, which is a cousin to humility, both of which will help connect you with the people who are listening to you. Sister Reyna I. Aburto of the Relief Society General Presidency endorsed the connecting power of sharing your weaknesses in an October 2019 general conference address. "Your struggles do not define you, but they can refine you," she said. "Because of a 'thorn in the flesh,' you may have the ability to feel more compassion toward others. As guided by the Holy Ghost, share your story in order to 'succor the weak, lift up the hands which hang down, and strengthen the feeble knees.'"[149]

Brené Brown, PhD, a social worker, spent six years studying why some people feel they're worthy of love and belonging and why others doubt their worth. She shared the answer in an insightful TED talk titled "The Power of Vulnerability." She says: People who have a strong sense of love and acceptance have the courage to be vulnerable. She explains her findings like this:

The original definition of courage, when it first came into the English language — it's from the Latin word "cor," meaning "heart" — and the original definition was to tell the story of who you are with your whole heart. And so these folks had, very simply, the courage to be imperfect...

The other thing they had in common was this: They fully embraced vulnerability. They believed that what made them vulnerable made them beautiful.

The point is: What makes you more vulnerable than standing up in front of 40 or 500 or 2,000 people with no written text to almost literally hide behind? Being vulnerable — or humble, or courageous — builds rapport with your audience. Losing your place or hemming and hawing, which may be terrifying, will increase your credibility and your audience's empathy. When you demonstrate your willingness to show your imperfect, honest self, your connection will be strengthened. Dr. Brown adds: "By the time you're a social worker for 10 years, what you realize is that connection is why we're here. It's what gives purpose and meaning to our lives."[150] And remember the spiritual benefits: "God's promise to the humble," said Elder Ulisses Soares, "is that He will lead them by the hand."[151]

Elder Gene R. Cook addresses the topic of not using a written text extensively in *Teaching By The Spirit*. He shares a story about when he was a newly returned missionary and spoke in several wards in his stake. After one talk — which went pretty well, he says — an older man approached him and said: "Brother Cook, why is it that you don't believe in teaching by the Spirit?"

Elder Cook was speechless. "I struggled with how to respond to him," he said, "and then said awkwardly, 'Well, I'm probably not as good at it as I should be, but I sure prayed over my talk and I tried to get prepared.'"

The old man continued to press him. He said, "You had your talk outlined in such perfect order that if the Lord had wanted to say something through you He wouldn't have had a chance."

Elder Cook says, "I was astonished. I didn't know what to say." But the next time he gave a talk, he followed that advice. Then he says:

From that day to this, I have never written a talk out unless I've been required to. I really do believe that if you believe, the Lord will speak through you to the needs of the people. I bear testimony that He will work with us as He did with Enoch when he said: "Go forth and do as I have commanded thee, and no man shall pierce thee. Open thy mouth, and it shall be filled, and I will give thee utterance, for all flesh is in my hands, and I will do as seemeth me good."

...Sometimes I've written down a few ideas, thoughts, stories, examples, illustrations, and some humor I might use, but it's been very loosely laid out on a sheet of paper. One would not be able to stand and read a talk from my notes.[152]

TRY IT NEXT TIME YOU SPEAK; SEE WHAT HAPPENS

My invitation: Try it. Judge the approach by its fruits. Come and see, as the Lord says.[153] Use an outline instead of a written sermon next time you speak and look at the faces of the people you're talking to during your talk. See how well you connect with them; listen to how the Lord guides your words. David O. McKay said in a 1907 general Sunday School conference that teachers who speak without depending on their texts "are free now to let the Spirit operate upon their intelligences, upon their souls."[154]

So try it — and see if you have the kind of experience Roger Terry described in an essay titled "The Lord Closed the Book."

On a spring evening in 1977, I learned a marvelous lesson about teaching by the Spirit. I was serving in West Berlin, Germany, and was working that day with Elder Selman, a missionary in my district. We had an appointment to teach the second discussion to the Ortlepps, a couple my companion and I had met while tracting. They had listened politely to the first discussion about Joseph Smith and the Restoration and had accepted our offer to teach them about the plan of salvation, even though we could tell they were not seriously interested.

When we knocked on their door, they invited us in, and the four of us took seats around their kitchen table. After engaging in some small talk, we opened with prayer. Back in the 1970s missionaries still memorized the discussions and presented them pretty much verbatim, and since I had been in the mission field for nearly two years, I knew them very well. In fact, when I would present the various concepts I could see the pages of the discussion book in my mind and would mentally turn the pages as I taught.

But on this particular evening the Lord had something different prepared for Herr and Frau Ortlepp. As I opened my mouth to speak, the Spirit took charge. It was as if the Lord reached out His hand and simply closed the discussion book in my mind. And as the book closed, a conduit opened — a spiritual connection between me and the Ortlepps. I somehow knew what they were thinking. I knew the questions they wanted to ask before they even had a chance to ask them. And using my voice, the Spirit gave them the answers they desired. I felt like a spectator as my voice taught them concepts I had never before understood. I knew without a doubt that the words I spoke specifically answered the questions and doubts they harbored in their hearts. A sweet spirit filled the room, and the Ortlepps were visibly moved.[155]

SOMEONE ELSE WILL BENEFIT WHEN YOU DON'T READ YOUR TALK — YOU

There's someone else who will benefit, besides the people who are listening to you, when you don't write out your talk: You. I've previously mentioned my friend David Meek, who's been a faithful proponent of President McKay's three principles in all his callings and talks over many years.

David sells commercial insurance for a living, and I asked him how he makes presentations to prospective clients. He said: "If I'm focused on my notes and not on the people in the room, I'm not effective. When I'm looking at my clients and making eye contact with them, we have a two-way connection that's good for both of us. I can look at someone and know they're listening to me, and if I'm looking at my next line I'm going to miss it."

I asked him: What happens at church when you rely too much on your script and don't establish that connection? "If you give a written talk and you read it well, people in the congregation may feel you gave a great talk," he said. "But really, the person who's robbed of the full impact of the talk is you." He paused for a moment, then said this with a degree of emotion: "Don't you get a thrill when you're up there speaking, and you get a spiritual impulse when you're speaking from your heart, and you're sharing not how you wrote something, but how you know it? There's communication going on not just between you and the congregation, but between you and the Lord."

Marion G. Romney confirmed David's point. He said: "I always know when I am speaking under the influence of the Holy Ghost because I always learn something from what I have said."[156]

My friend David continued: "In order to expand on two-way communication and in order to be guided by the Spirit, I want to look at people and see their expressions. You can look at someone and see how they're receiving what they're hearing. That helps you as a speaker. It might make you more receptive about where you should go and what you should emphasize. If you're trying to speak by the Spirit, that's probably a lot better way of helping you listen to those promptings. You're not bound to your words on the page. You're in the moment."

In spiritual settings, the impact David is talking about can mirror what happened to Stephen when he preached to a crowed of people in a synagogue in Jerusalem, as described in Acts 6:10: "And they were not able to resist the wisdom and the spirit by which he spake."

ADVICE FROM THREE EXPERTS
ABOUT NOT READING YOUR TALK VERBATIM

Here are three strong arguments — one secular, two spiritual — against reading a written speech. First is a vigorous endorsement from Tom Peters, a business consultant, author, and nationally prominent lecturer. In his book on management and organizational improvement titled *The Pursuit of WOW*, he includes this advice in a list of pointers on how to give effective presentations:

> For heaven's sake, don't write (your presentation) out! If spontaneity isn't everything, it verges on it. That hardly means winging it. Paradoxically, careful preparation breeds comfort and thence spawns spontaneity. In short, never, ever write it out in full. If you do, you become a slave to your exact wording and inevitably lose 75 percent [make that 90, 95, 97 percent] of any emotional impact.[158]

Anyone who's listened to speakers read their PowerPoint slides in a business meeting can vouch for Peters's point: Reading your talk robs you of your emotional connection to your audience.

Second, here's a spiritual rationale — an explanation of the power of letting the Lord guide your words in the very moment you speak — from Elder Bruce R. McConkie in his book *Mormon Doctrine*. The entry on sermons says:

> There may be a few instances in which sermons may be read, just as there are a few formal occasions when prayers may be read, as for instance at the dedication of temples. On some radio and television broadcasts written sermons may be appropriate, and there is no impropriety in little children reading written talks. But in the absence of some compelling reason for doing so, those privileged to deliver gospel sermons should: 1. Treasure up those principles of light and

truth which it is appropriate to teach from time to time; 2. Manifest sufficient faith to rely on the Lord for guidance as the occasion requires; and 3. Cultivate the ability to attune themselves to the promptings and whisperings of the Spirit when actually standing before the people.

Every experienced elder has spoken on occasions when the spirit of inspiration has rested upon him, when by the power of the Holy Ghost thoughts have come into his mind, and words have fallen from his lips, which were new to him. Many direct revelations are given to the Lord's agents as they stand on their feet, relying on the Spirit, preaching the gospel.[159]

And third, Elder Gene R. Cook shared his testimony in *Teaching By The Spirit* about the Lord's ability to help you know what to say — if you'll trust him:

[The Lord] can inspire you directly from heaven with things you do not know, and thus teach you in the process as well. He can touch your heart while you are teaching, and that will cause others to feel the message more fully. He can bless the people with the Holy Ghost so they will leave the meeting committed to better follow Jesus Christ and purify their lives.

All of that comes about as a result of true teaching by the Spirit. I bear testimony that it works. This is the Lord's kingdom. This is his gospel. These are his teachings. He surely knows how to convey them and is more able to do so as we become more open and flexible and trusting that he will speak through us.

I bear testimony that the simplest soul can do what I have just described. It is not a matter of how much you know. It is a matter of whether or not you are willing to humble yourself and believe that the Lord will speak through you, willing to prepare yourself as an instrument, and then willing to give him that opportunity, despite the feeling of risk to yourself — the risk of failing, of not doing well, of being awkward in your sentence structure, of stumbling over yourself.

If those feelings of risk are replaced with true faith, I testify that the Lord will speak through his servants — men, women, and children — and the message will better reach the hearts of his people.[160]

So consider the Lord's advice throughout the scriptures — in D&C 84:85, Matthew 10:19-20, Luke 12:11-12, Luke 21:14, and D&C 100:6 — and ask yourself: Do I think the Lord will help me know what I should say when I stand up to speak, in the very moment when I need his help? And do I think he'll help me not only in what I say, but in how I say it?

Think of this example. When Joseph F. Smith was on his way home to Utah in 1857 after his mission in Hawaii, he was accosted by a band of ruffians who were threatening to kill any Latter-day Saints they found. It was a frightening time. Opposition to the Church was sanctioned by the U.S. government, and persecution and acts of violence against members of the Church were common. The marauders charged into Elder Smith's camp, scattered his travel companions, and confronted him. The leader of the gang pointed a pistol at Elder Smith's head, cursed, and asked him: "Are you a Mormon?"

My guess is Elder Smith was more nervous than you've ever been when you're sitting on the stand waiting to give a talk. But in the very moment when his life was on the line, the young returned missionary smiled at the gunman and boldly said the words that flashed into his mind: "Yesiree! Dyed in the wool, true blue, through and through."

Everything stopped. The hooligan was dumbfounded. Then he uncocked his pistol. "Well," he said. "You are the blankety-blankedest pleasantest man I ever met! Shake hands, young fellow. I am glad to see a man that stands up for his convictions."

The man climbed back on his horse and rode away, followed by his gang.[161]
And note: Elder Smith responded without writing out what he said.

FOUR SAMPLE OUTLINES

If you use President McKay's three principles — and if you agree to try not writing out your talk — what will your notes look like? You may be so comfortable writing your talks word for word that you don't have any idea how to speak from an outline. Remember Elder Cook's experience: "Sometimes I've written down a few ideas, thoughts, stories, examples, illustrations, and some humor I might use, *but it's been very loosely laid out on a sheet of paper. One would not be able to stand and read a talk from my notes.*"[162]

Here are four examples that may give you an idea of how to format your notes:

EXAMPLE 1: YOU'VE BEEN ASKED TO SPEAK IN SACRAMENT MEETING ON FAITH. You have 15 minutes, and your notes could look like this:

1. My objective is to tell you how faith has made a difference in my life.
2. Faith has two components — belief plus action — and both of those components are essential in order to generate enough faith to enhance our lives
   - Hebrews 11: 1 and 33-34
3. Why belief is important:
   - Story: Sitting by the girl from California in freshman English at BYU-Idaho: "Hi. Come here often?"
   - Whitney L. Clayton, April 2015 general conference: "Belief and testimony and faith are not passive principles. They do not just happen to us. Belief is something we choose — we hope for it, we work for it, and we sacrifice for it. We will not accidentally come to believe in the Savior and His gospel any more than we will accidentally pray or pay tithing. We actively choose to believe, just like we choose to keep other commandments."
   - Enos 3-4

4. Why action is important:
   - Story: The difference between taking a young friend on visits when I was bishop instead of lecturing him while we sat in the bishop's office
   - Alma 36: 16-20
   - Dieter F. Uchtdorf, April 2011 general conference: "Often, the answer to our prayer does not come while we're on our knees but while we're on our feet serving the Lord and serving those around us. Selfless acts of service and consecration refine our spirits, remove the scales from our spiritual eyes, and open the windows of heaven. By becoming the answer to someone's prayer, we often find the answer to our own."
5. Combining belief plus action increases our faith and strengthens our connection to the Lord's Spirit.
   - Story: Boyd K. Packer looks for a home when he moves to Salt Lake City...
6. D&C 123: 16-17: "A very large ship is benefited very much by a very small helm in the time of a storm, by being kept workways with the wind and the waves. Therefore, dearly beloved brethren, let us cheerfully do all things that lie in our power; and then may we stand still, with the utmost assurance, to see the salvation of God, and for his arm to be revealed."
7. Testimony/close

EXAMPLE 2: YOU'VE BEEN ASKED TO SPEAK IN STAKE CONFERENCE ABOUT THE SCRIPTURES. You have 10 minutes.

1. Objective: The scriptures are a blessing in my day-to-day life because I gained a testimony of them when I was young — and because I've made it a habit to read them every day.
   a. I learned two things from the Book of Mormon when I read it the first time:
      i. First, it's true

      ii. Second, wickedness never was happiness

2. Two experiences when I was a teenager:
   a. Story: I learned that wickedness never was happiness by sluffing seminary when I was in ninth grade
   b. Story: One of my friends learned that wickedness never was happiness when we were kids (and one didn't)
3. The scriptures will only bless your life if you read them
   a. My process for daily scripture study
4. Robert D. Hales, October 2006 general conference: "When we want to speak to God, we pray. And when we want Him to speak to us, we search the scriptures."
5. Testimony/close

EXAMPLE 3: YOU'RE CONDUCTING A STAKE MEETING THAT'S BEEN A LITTLE UNFOCUSED AND DULL. You sense you ought to add some spiritual oomph before the meeting ends.

1. Think of a brief example in your life that strengthened your testimony of the principle the meeting has been addressing.
2. If you can think of a scripture that reiterates your example, quote it or paraphrase it.
3. Bear your testimony, then close the meeting with a charge to apply what you've discussed.

EXAMPLE 4: YOU'RE ASKED TO SPEAK AT A YOUNG ADULT FIRESIDE ON DATING. This one makes you squirm, in part because you're supposed to speak for 45 minutes. Plus thinking about dating makes you feel like you're 16 again; it still gives you sweaty palms.

Then you have a happy thought: You think maybe you're coming down with a cold. You're going to be sick — hopefully *very* sick — which means it's okay to turn down the talk. But you cough, and the cough is obviously fake. So…you're stuck. You take a deep breath, then make an outline that looks like this:

1. **MY POINT:** Dating is important, because without it, it's hard to get married.
   a. Spencer W. Kimball: "Successful marriage depends in large measure upon the preparation made in approaching it…One cannot pick the ripe, luscious fruit from a tree that was never planted, nurtured, nor pruned."
   b. So here are four steps that help you date successfully, which I learned by painful experience.
2. **STEP 1:** Remember Nike's advice: Just do it — because the Spirit comes in the doing, as Elder Hartman Rector, Junior, said.
   a. Story: Homecoming dances in high school…versus freshman year in college.
   b. You get good at what you practice: Asking Laurie out in December 1979…
      i. Once we went out once or twice, it started to be fun to talk on the phone.
      ii. And talking on the phone made it easier to keep going out.
   c. Pay attention to what you learn along the way — especially to insights about character.
      i. Dad's advice about Laurie.
3. **STEP 2:** God grants unto us according to our desires — Alma 29:4.
   a. You get what you really want —
   b. And you identify what you really want by identifying it and working at it.
      i. Story: Emily/Paul praying, 1985ish: Bless Dad to take us to the park...
      ii. Story: How Heber J. Grant learned to throw a baseball: "That which we persist in doing becomes easier for us to do — not that the nature of the thing is changed, but that our power to

do is increased."

4. STEP 3: Remember the Jacob 6:12 rule: Be wise.

   a. Story: How Heber J. Grant kept trying to learn to sing...and never succeeded.

   b. Story: My prayer about Laurie in the Salt Lake Temple, May 1980.

5. STEP 4: Learn how to converse effectively.

   a. Conversation is the currency of relationships — the better you are at it, the more successful you'll be in dating and in your relationships.

   b. How?

      i. Ask questions, really listen, then ask follow-up questions.

      ii. The more you talk about yourself, the less interesting you'll be.

      iii. Example: Bitter divorced guy in the job interview...

   c. Story: Talking with Paul on the way to work, 2001.

   d. Story: Talking with Laurie about how she decided in high school about what kind of boy she wanted to marry.

      i. Laurie: I didn't want to marry an athlete.

      ii. Me: But I *am* an athlete!

6. So dating leads to marriage — and what's the result of a happy marriage?

   a. Joseph Smith to Emma in *Rough Stone Rolling*, page 186: He wrote to say he wanted time with her "to converse with you on all the subjects which concern us."

      i. Quote: "The letter suggests a marriage where everything was talked over — the family, the gossip, church problems, and Joseph's inward battles."

   b. Boyd K. Packer, April 2015 general conference: "If you suppose that the full-blown rapture of young romantic love is the sum total of the possibilities which spring from the fountains of life, you have not yet lived to see the devotion and the comfort of longtime married love. Married couples are tried by temptation, misunderstandings, financial problems, family crises, and illness, and all the while love grows stronger. Mature love has a bliss not even imagined by newlyweds."

8. Testimony/close

NEAL MAXWELL'S ADVICE: CREATE A FLIGHT PLAN

Neal A. Maxwell had the perfect metaphor for the kind of planning I'm trying to describe: Rather than writing a speech, you're creating a flight plan. In a 1991 talk to seminary teachers titled "Teaching by the Spirit — The Language of Inspiration" (which is very much worth looking up and reading in its entirety), he said:

> Teaching by the Spirit is not the equivalent of going on "automatic pilot." We still need a carefully worked out flight plan. Studying out something in our own minds involves the Spirit in our preparations as well as in our presentations. We must not err, like Oliver Cowdery, by taking no thought except to ask God for his Spirit (see D&C 9:7).
>
> Seeking the Spirit is best done when we ask the Lord to take the lead of an already informed mind, in which things have been "studied out." Additionally, if we already care deeply about those to be taught, it is so much easier for the Lord to inspire us to give customized counsel and emphasis to those we teach. Thus we can not be clinically detached when teaching by the Spirit.[163]

Here are two final stories that illustrate two final points I want to emphasize.

First is a three-part experience I had when I was teaching a group of energetic 11-year-olds in Primary. Part one of the story was a lesson

CLARIFYING QUESTIONS: DELIVERING THE MESSAGE

*Share your answers and see what others
have posted at BetterTalksLDS.com.*

1. Which would you rather hear — a talk that's written out or one that's delivered extemporaneously?

2. What differences have you noticed in a talk that's read verbatim and one that's delivered only from notes?

3. When have you benefitted from being vulnerable? How did your vulnerability affect the people or person you were talking to?

4. What can you do to deal with the fear you'll face if your talk isn't written out word-for-word in advance?

5. When have you spoken from your heart — not from your text — in a talk, and how did it affect you and the people you were addressing?

6. Look at a talk you've delivered previously that was completely written out in advance. How would you turn it into an outline?

TWO FINAL EXPERIENCES
(AND THE LESSONS THEY TAUGHT ME)

I taught on the martyrdom of Stephen, which I illustrated by dumping a box of baseball-sized rocks onto the floor. *Pick one up*, I told the kids. They did. I said: *Now throw them at each other.* They looked at me. The normal beehivish buzz of our class stopped dead.

I said: *I'm kidding!*

I had an objective. I shared (and asked the class members to share) examples. I emphasized application. We talked about Stephen's testimony, and I shared my testimony. We talked about what we'd do if they were in a position like Stephen's. I asked: Would you deny your testimony in order to save your life? What situations would you encounter that would tempt you to not be true to what you know is right? The lesson was okay; the kids were more-or-less engaged. But it wasn't great. There wasn't the spiritual oomph I'd been hoping for the kids to experience. Plus once everyone put down their rocks, my partner fell asleep, and he slept through the entire lesson. *Oh well*, I thought when the lesson was over. *Sometimes you win, sometimes you snooze.*

Part two of the story: The next week, it was my partner's turn to teach, and he taught the *exact same lesson*. He lost track of which lesson to teach. He didn't use rocks to tell the story of Stephen and he didn't ask any questions about similar situations the kids would face. We didn't have much of a discussion. In fact the kids were comatose through much of the lesson — and I struggled to stay engaged myself. I thought: *It would be kind of funny if I slept through this whole lesson, just like my partner did last week,* and as the lesson dragged on I thought: *Plus it would be* really *easy.*

And during the lesson, no one said: *Hey, this is what we talked about last week.* Not a peep about the rerun. The kids — who were normally quick to point out any inconsistencies in our lessons — didn't notice it.

Here's part three of the story: Toward the end of my partner's lesson, one of the kids — who was very bright, but usually one of our class's most disruptive, most easily distracted members — mentioned a scripture he'd read while my partner had been slogging through the lesson. I believe it was Acts 6:3, which describes what Stephen and the members of the Seventy were like: "Honest...full of the Holy Ghost and wisdom."

He read the scripture and said: That's the kind of people who are leaders of the Church today. And as he spoke, the Spirit, capital S, was there. *The Spirit that had eluded us the week before when I'd taught the same lesson reinforced his words; it edified me and everyone in the room.* It was incredible — and I was amazed. I walked out of the classroom thinking: As teachers, we can control the things we can control, but the Lord controls the Spirit — and the Spirit is the only way we really learn the principles of the gospel. Henry B. Eyring described what my young friend in Primary did at the end of our tedious lesson:

I urge all of us, young and old, who are called to speak in a meeting in the name of the Lord to dismiss our feelings of self-doubt and inadequacy. We don't have to use soaring language or convey deep insights. Simple words of testimony will do. The Spirit will give you the words for you to speak and will carry them down into the hearts of humble people who look for truth from God. If we keep trying to speak for the Lord, we will be surprised someday to learn that we have warned, exhorted, taught, and invited with the help of the Spirit to bless lives, with power far beyond our own.[164]

The lesson I hope you'll take away from the story is this: You don't have to be a great orator or a skilled teacher to speak with impact in the Kingdom of God. You just have to have the Spirit. President Eyring described what happened perfectly: Our young class member spoke with power far beyond his own. Doctrine and Covenants 42:27 says: "If ye receive not the Spirit ye shall not teach." President Eyring added this thought in an April 2016 conference talk: "I have learned that the only exhortation that changes hearts comes from the Holy Ghost."[165] David O. McKay's three principles don't matter; nothing matters except the Lord's Spirit.

Remember this: If you have the Spirit of God, your talk or your lesson or discussion will make a difference. If you don't, no matter how interesting your comments are, it won't.

One more story. The spring of 2007 was an exceptionally busy time for me at work, where I was involved in a massive project that required me to invest 15 or 20 hours of overtime every week. The project was going to last for almost the entire year, and the stress I was feeling seeped into every aspect of my life. It was easy to be impatient and overwhelmed and to complain about the demands of my schedule. I worked most evenings and parts of many Saturdays.

But on the first weekend of April, I was listening to the Saturday morning session of general conference. Jeffrey R. Holland was speaking. He gave a talk titled "The Tongue of Angels," which covers being positive in thought and word. Part of what Elder Holland said jumped out at me: "We should honor the Savior's declaration to 'be of good cheer,'" he said. "Indeed, it seems to me we may be more guilty of breaking that commandment than almost any other! Speak hopefully. Speak encouragingly, including about yourself. Try not to complain and moan incessantly. As someone once said, 'Even in the golden age of civilization someone undoubtedly grumbled that everything looked too yellow.'"

As I heard those words, I thought: *He's talking to* me *about how I act and what I say at work — and at church and at home.* I didn't take Elder Holland's words as reproof; instead I remember being filled with a jolt of pure joy. I thought as I sat there and listened: *The Lord knows me so well that he knows what I need to hear — and he's using Elder Holland to give it to me.* Elder Holland closed his address by saying this:

I pray that my words, even on this challenging subject, will be encouraging to you, not discouraging, that you can hear in my voice that I love you, because I do. More importantly, please know that your Father in Heaven loves you and so does His Only Begotten Son. When They speak to you — and They will — it will not be in the wind, nor in the earthquake, nor in the fire, but it will be with a voice still and small, a voice tender and kind. It will be with the tongue of angels.[166]

I felt that love Elder Holland described; it encircled me in a warm, powerful, personal embrace. That feeling told me: *Rich, relax. Things will be okay.* I wrote in my journal: "I was *thrilled.* It's a great feeling to know the Lord knows exactly what I need — and that we have a guy like Elder Holland who can verbalize it for us." His advice helped me cope with that demanding year, and it's helped me ever since. If you go back and read the talk, you'll see its impact, but you'll have to realize it may not help you, because it seemed like it was only meant for *me.*

I felt, in other words, what Solomon described in Proverbs 10:11: "The mouth of a righteous man is a well of life." I drank from that well that morning, and I've never forgotten it. A good speech — delivered with the Lord's Spirit — has that kind of power.

That's why learning to speak effectively is important: Because we all need that living water every time we go to church, or visit a fellow saint, or talk with a family member or anyone in need.

BIBLIOGRAPHY

BOOKS

Richard N. Armstrong, *The Rhetoric of David O. McKay, Mormon Prophet,* New York, Peter Lang Press, 1993, pages 119, 123-124.

———, Church Handbook of Instructions, Book 2: Priesthood and Auxiliary Leaders, The Church of Jesus Christ of Latter-day Saints, Salt Lake City, 1998, page 304.

Ezra Taft Benson, *Teachings of Ezra Taft Benson,* Bookcraft, Salt Lake City, 1988, page 384, based on a speech he gave at a mission presidents' seminar, June 27, 1974.

Benson Bobrick, *Wide as the Waters: The Story of the English Bible and the Revolution It Inspired,* New York, Simon & Schuster, 2001, https://books.google.com/books?id= lvyKnhiavIMC&pg=PT62&dq=quotes,+lancelot+andrewes,+%22left+abandoned% 22&hl=en&sa=X&ved=0ahUKEwjxhNz31ZfPAhVGwiYKHRbNAioQ6AEIH jAA#v=onepage&q=quotes%2C%20lancelot%20andrewes%2C%20%22left%20 abandoned%22&f=false.

Book of Mormon, 1 Nephi 19:23, Mosiah 2:9, Alma 32:28, Alma 36: 17-21.

———, *Come, Follow Me — For Individuals and Families,* The Church of Jesus Christ of Latter-day Saints, 2019 and 2020.

Gene R. Cook, *Teaching By The Spirit,* Salt Lake City, © Deseret Book Company, 2000, pages 37-41, 64, 65, 73-74, 78, 91, 122-123, 124, 125, 181.

Stephen R. Covey, *The Seven Habits of Highly Effective People,* New York, Simon and Schuster, 1989, pages 30-31, 98, 319.

Stephen R. Covey, *Spiritual Roots of Human Relations,* Deseret Book, Salt Lake City, Utah, 1977, pages 8, 51-52, 161-163, 254.

Scott C. Esplin and Richard Neitzel Holzapfel, *The Voice of My Servants: Apostolic Messages on Teaching, Learning, and Scripture,* Salt Lake City, Deseret Book, 2010, chapter 1: Thomas S. Monson, "How to Communicate Effectively," https://rsc.byu.edu/archived/ voice-my-servants/how-communicate-effectively, pages 3-10.

Clifton Fadman, *The Little, Brown Book of Anecdotes,* Boston, 1985, page 140.

BIBLIOGRAPHY

Bruce C. Hafen, *A Disciple's Life*, Salt Lake City, Deseret Book, 2002, page 290.

Leon R. Hartshorn, *Outstanding Stories by General Authorities Volume III*, Deseret Book, 1975, page 177; devotional address at Brigham Young University-Idaho by Sheri L. Dew, "True Blue, Through and Through," March 16, 2004; Preparation of Joseph F. Smith, "True Blue, Through and Through," https://www.youtube.com/watch?v=TEKiOH-cIbU.

Jeffrey R. Holland, *Trusting Jesus*, Salt Lake City, Deseret Book, 2003, pages 155-157.

———, *Hymns of The Church of Jesus Christ of Latter-day Saints*, 1985, page 241.

———, *Journal of Discourses*, 1: 90-91.

———, *Journal of Discourses*, 4: 368.

Bruce R. McConkie, *Doctrinal New Testament Commentary*, 3:246–47, Salt Lake City, Deseret Book, 2002.

Bruce R. McConkie, *Mormon Doctrine*, Second Edition, Salt Lake City, Bookcraft, 1966, pages 703-704.

Joseph Fielding McConkie, *The Bruce R. McConkie Story: Reflections of a Son*, Salt Lake City, Deseret Book, 2003, pages 9, 255

New Testament, Mark 5:19, Luke 8:39, John 1:39, Acts 14:27.

Boyd K. Packer, *Teach Ye Diligently*, Salt Lake City, Deseret Book, 1979, pages 71, 304, 354-355.

Pearl of Great Price, Moses 6:32, Joseph Smith History 1:12-13.

Thomas J. Peters and Robert H. Waterman, *In Search of Excellence*, New York, Warner Books, 1982, pages 61, 62.

Tom Peters, *The Pursuit of Wow*, New York, Vintage Books, 1994, pages 288-289.

Tom Peters, *Thriving on Chaos*, New York, Perennial Library/Harper & Row, 1988, pages 506 and 587.

Gregory A. Prince and Wm. Robert Wright, *David O. McKay and the Rise of Modern Mormonism*, Salt Lake City, University of Utah Press, 2005, pages 3, 29.

James E. Talmage, *Jesus the Christ*, Salt Lake City, published by The Church of Jesus Christ of Latter-day Saints, 1981, pages 140, 141, 151 [including the notes to chapter 11, note number 4]; "He Spake Many Things Unto them in Parables," pages 295, 297, and 299.

Lucile C. Tate, *Boyd K. Packer: A Watchman on the Tower*, Salt Lake City, Bookcraft, 1995, page 145; taken from an interview with Dr. Steven Smith, February 2, 1990.

———, *Teaching, No Greater Call*, The Church of Jesus Christ, Salt Lake City, 1999, pages vii and 98, 180.

TALKS AND ARTICLES

Richard Lloyd Anderson "How to Read a Parable," September 1974 *Ensign*, https://www.lds.org/ensign/1974/09/how-to-read-a-parable?lang=eng.

———, AZ Quotes, Wolfgang Amadeus Mozart, http://www.azquotes.com/quote/555629.

M. Russell Ballard, "President Gordon B. Hinckley," *Ensign* magazine, September 1994, page 9.

James H. Bekker, address at Parleys Stake conference, January 11, 2020.

Brené Brown, "The Power of Vulnerability, http://brenebrown.com/.

———, LDS Church News, April 20, 2013.

———, LDS Church News, July 7, 2012, Seminar for new mission presidents, June 25, 2012, http://www.ldschurchnewsarchive.com/articles/62513/Seminar-for-mission-presidents--Lord-will-go-before-you.html.

Whitney L. Clayton, Blog on Family Search, September 9, 2015, "Teach People, Not Lessons, https://familysearch.org/blog/en/elder-clayton-teach-people-lessons/.

———, Conference Report, April 1912, page 52.

Quentin L. Cook, "Restoring Morality and Religious Freedom," December 2011 commencement address at BYU-Idaho, September 2012 Ensign, https://www.lds.org/ensign/2012/09/restoring-morality-and-religious-freedom?lang=eng.

BIBLIOGRAPHY

Elaine S. Dalton, "Be Not Moved!", General Young Women's Meeting, March 20, 2013, https://www.lds.org/general-conference/2013/04/be-not-moved?lang=eng.

Henry B. Eyring, "Eternal Families," April 2016 general conference, https://www.lds.org/general-conference/2016/04/eternal-families?lang=eng&_r=1.

Henry B. Eyring, "Serve with the Spirit," October 2010 general conference,https://www.lds.org/general-conference/2010/10serve-with-the-spirit?lang=eng&_r=1.

Henry B. Eyring, "Write Upon My Heart," October 2000 general conference, reprinted in the November 2000 Ensign, page 87, https://www.lds.org/general-conference/2000/10/write-upon-my-heart?lang=eng&_r=1.

———, Golf Digest, April 26, 2016, "Innovators and Influencers of 2016," http://www.golfdigest.com/story/innovators-and-influencers-of-2016.

———, GoodReads (and numerous other internet references) http://www.goodreads.com/quotes/162599-according-to-most-studies-people-s-number-one-fear-is-public.

Allen D. Haynie, "Remembering In Whom We Have Trusted, October 2015 general conference, https://www.lds.org/ensign/2015/11/sunday-afternoon-session/remembering-in-whom-we-have-trusted?lang=eng.

George R. Hill, "President David O. McKay, Father of the Modern Sunday School," Instructor, September 1960, page 313.

John Hilton III and Mindy Raye Friedman, "Speaking in Sacrament Meeting," New Era, October 2011, https://abn.churchofjesuschrist.org/study/new-era/2011/10/speaking-in-sacrament-meeting?lang=eng

Gordon B. Hinckley, "A Charter for Youth," Conference Report, October 1965, page 52.

Gordon B. Hinckley, "How to Be a Teacher When Your Role as a Leader Requires You to Teach," General Authority Priesthood Board Meeting, February 5, 1969.

Gordon B. Hinckley, "Take Not the Name of God in Vain," October 1987 general conference, https://www.lds.org/general-conference/1987/10/take-not-the-name-of-god-in-vain?lang=eng&_r=1.

Jeffrey R. Holland, "For Times of Trouble," devotional address at BYU, March 18, 1980, https://speeches.byu.edu/talks/jeffrey-r-holland_times-trouble/.

Jeffrey R. Holland, "The Tongue of Angels," April 2007 general conference, https://www.lds.org/general-conference/2007/04/the-tongue-of-angels?lang=eng&_r=1.

Martin Luther King, Junior, "I Have A Dream," delivered on August 28, 1963, https://www.npr.org/2010/01/18/122701268/i-have-a-dream-speech-in-its-entirety

The Instructor, September 1960, page 314.

The Juvenile Instructor, April 15, 1905, "The Lesson Aim: How to Select It, How to Develop It, How to Apply It," page 242; May 1, 1907, volume 42, page 38.

Merlin R. Lybbert, "A Latter-day Samaritan," April 1990 general conference, https://www.lds.org/general-conference/1990/04/a-latter-day-samaritan?lang=eng.

James O. Mason, "A New Health Missionary Program, October 1971 general conference, https://www.lds.org/ensign/1971/12/a-new-health-missionary-program?lang=eng.

Neal A. Maxwell, "Called and Prepared from the Foundation of the World," April 1986 general conference, https://www.lds.org/general-conference/1986/04/called-and-prepared-from-the-foundation-of-the-world?lang=eng.

Neal A. Maxwell, "Teaching by the Spirit — The Language of Inspiration," CES Symposium on the Old Testament, August 15, 1991, Teaching Seminary Preservice Readings Religion 370, 471, and 475, (2004), 35-40, https://www.lds.org/manual/teaching-seminary-preservice-readings-religion-370-471-and-475/teaching-by-the-spirit-the-language-of-inspiration?lang=eng.

Bruce R. McConkie, "The How and Why of Faith-Promoting Stories," *New Era,* July 1978, page 5.

Bruce R. McConkie, "The Purifying Power of Gethsemane," April 1985, https://www.lds.org/general-conference/1985/04/the-purifying-power-of-gethsemane?lang=eng.
———, "David O. McKay, Ambassador of the Faith," *Ensign,* January 2005.

David O. McKay, "Harmony in the Home," general conference address, Friday, April 6, 1956; published in the Conference Report, April 1956, page 4. https://archive.org/

stream/conferencereport1956a#page/n9/mode/1uphttps://www.lds.org/ensign/
1985/03/principles?lang=eng.

Harrison Monarth, "The Irresistible Power of Storytelling as a Strategic Business Tool,"
Harvard Business Review, March 11, 2014.

Thomas S. Monson, "Examples of Righteousness," April 2008 general conference,
https://www.lds.org/general-conference/2008/04/examples-of-righteousness?
lang=eng&_r=1.

Thomas S. Monson, "Thou Art a Teacher Come From God," Conference Report, October
1970 general conference, pages 104-108, http://scriptures.byu.edu/gettalk.php?ID=1811.

————, News at Princeton, posted December 5, 2011; https://www.princeton.edu/main/
news/archive/S32/27/76E76/index.xml?section=featured

Dallin H. Oaks, "The Challenge to Become," October 2000 general conference, https://
www.lds.org/general-conference/2000/10/the-challenge-to-become?lang=eng&_r=1.

Dallin H. Oaks, "Gospel Teaching," October 1999 general conference,
https://www.lds.org/general-conference/1999/10/gospel-teaching?lang=eng.

Boyd K. Packer, "The Candle of the Lord," https://www.lds.org/ensign/1983/01/
the-candle-of-the-lord?lang=eng, June 25, 1982.

Boyd K. Packer, "Inspiring Music, Worthy Thoughts," delivered in October 1973 general
conference; printed in the January 1974 *Ensign,* https://www.lds.org/ensign/1974/01/
inspiring-music-worthy-thoughts?lang=eng.

Boyd K. Packer, "Principles," an address given on April 6, 1984, at a regional representatives'
seminar; summarized in the *Ensign,* March 1985; https://www.lds.org/ensign/1985/
03/principles?lang=eng.

Quoted by Boyd K. Packer in "Teach the Children," *Ensign,* February 2000,
https://www.lds.org/ensign/2000/02/teach-the-children?lang=eng.

Boyd K. Packer, "The Word of Wisdom: The Principle and the Promise," *Ensign,*
May 1996, page 17.

BIBLIOGRAPHY

Bonnie D. Parkin, "Remember Who You Are!," BYU fireside address, March 7, 2004, https://speeches.byu.edu/talks/bonnie-d-parkin/remember/

Bonnie L. Oscarson, "Defenders of the Family Proclamation," General Women's Session, March 28, 2015, https://www.lds.org/general-conference/2015/04/defenders-of-the-family-proclamation?lang=eng.

Russell T. Osguthorpe, "One Step Closer to the Savior," October 2012 general conference, https://www.lds.org/general-conference/2012/10/one-step-closer-to-the-savior?lang=eng.

L. Tom Perry, "Making the Right Decisions," general conference, October 1979, https://www.lds.org/general-conference/1979/10/making-the-right-decisions?lang=eng.

Matthew O. Richardson, "Teaching After the Manner of the Spirit," October 2011, https://www.lds.org/general-conference/2011/10/teaching-after-the-manner-of-the-spirit?lang=eng&_r=1.

Marion G. Romney, "First Presidency Message: Principles of Temporal Salvation," April 1981 *Ensign*, https://www.lds.org/ensign/1981/04/principles-of-temporal-salvation?lang=eng.

Richard G. Scott, "Acquiring Spiritual Knowledge," https://www.lds.org/general-conference/1993/10/acquiring-spiritual-knowledge?lang=eng&_r=1,

———, *Sports Illustrated*, "The Evolution of the Left Tackle," September 25, 2006, pages 59 and 60.

Vaiangina Sikahema, "Our Religious Obligation to be Educated," devotional address at BYU-Hawaii, delivered on January 14, 2020, https://speeches.byuh.edu/devotional/our-religious-obligation-to-be-educated

Ulisses Soares, "Be Meek and Lowly of Heart," October 2013 general conference, https://www.lds.org/general-conference/2013/10/be-meek-and-lowly-of-heart?lang=eng Russell C. Taylor, "The Joy of Service," October 1984 general conference, https://www.lds.org/general-conference/1984/10/the-joy-of-service?lang=eng&_r=1.

Benjamin M. Z. Tai, "The Power of the Book of Mormon in Conversion," April 2020 general conference, https://www.churchofjesuschrist.org/study/general-conference/2020/04/27tai?lang=eng

BIBLIOGRAPHY

Teachings of Heber J. Grant, The Church of Jesus Christ of Latter-day Saints, chapter 4; taken from the April 1939 Conference Report, page 18, https://www.lds.org/manual/teachings-heber-j-grant/chapter-4?lang=eng.

Teachings of Joseph Smith, lesson manual, chapter 24: Leading in the Lord's Way, https://www.lds.org/manual/teachings-joseph-smith/chapter-24?lang=eng#3-36481_000_028

Teachings of the Presidents of the Church xxviii, quoted in the Ensign, January 2005, in "David O. McKay, Ambassador of the Faith."

Michael John U. Teh, "The Power of the Word of God," March 2013 *Ensign*, https://www.lds.org/ensign/2013/03/the-power-of-the-word-of-god?lang=eng.

———, "The Lord Closed the Book," *Ensign*, February 2006, https://www.lds.org/ensign/2006/02/the-lord-closed-the-book?lang=eng.

Dieter F. Uchtdorf, "The Merciful Obtain Mercy," April 2012 general conference, https://www.lds.org/general-conference/2012/04/the-merciful-obtain-mercy?lang=eng.

Dieter F. Uchtdorf, "The Why of Priesthood Service," April 2012 general conference, https://www.lds.org/general-conference/2012/04/the-why-of-priesthood-service?lang=eng.

———, "'I Have a Dream' Leads Top 100 Speeches of the Century," University of Wisconsin-Madison, December 15, 1999, https://news.wisc.edu/i-have-a-dream-leads-top-100-speeches-of-the-century/

———, "We Believe in Being True," *Improvement Era*, Sept. 1959, page 647.

———, "The Wondrous and True Story of Christmas: First Presidency Message," December 2000 *Ensign*, https://www.lds.org/ensign/2000/12/the-wondrous-and-true-story-of-christmas?lang=eng.

Rosemary M. Wixom, "Discovering the Divinity Within," October 2015 general conference, https://www.lds.org/general-conference/2015/10/discovering-the-divinity-within?lang=eng.

WordWrite Communications, posted by Paul Furiga, April 16, 2013; http://www.wordwritepr.com/Blog/bid/114895/The-science-that-proves-the-effectiveness-of-storytelling-in-business.

PERSONAL RESOURCES

Conversation with Nathan Y. Jarvis, winter 2005.

Conversation with David H. Meek, February 2016, August 17, 2016.

Conversation with Mark J. Ott, MD, November 2015.

Conversation with Blair M. Kent, May 2020.

Email sent by H. Gary Pehrson, December 21, 2009.

Training class attended by the author, Intermountain Health Care central office, July 11, 1995.

Written testimony by Heather H. Barth, personal collection of the author.

FOOTNOTES

[1] Stephen R. Covey, *Spiritual Roots of Human Relations,* Deseret Book, Salt Lake City, Utah, 1977, pages 161-163.

[2] Richard G. Scott, "Acquiring Spiritual Knowledge," https://www.lds.org/general-conference/1993/10/acquiring-spiritual-knowledge?lang=eng&_r=1,

[3] Boyd K. Packer, "The Word of Wisdom: The Principle and the Promise," Ensign, May 1996, page 17.

[4] Boyd K. Packer, "Principles," an address given on April 6, 1984, at 1985; https://www.lds.org/ensign/1985/03/principles?lang=eng.

[5] *Come, Follow Me — For Individuals and Families,* published by The Church of Jesus Christ of Latter-day Saints, 2018, page 120 of print edition, https://www.lds.org/study/manual/come-follow-me-for-individuals-and-families-new-testament-2019/30?lang=eng.

[6] "David O. McKay, Ambassador of the Faith," *Ensign,* January 2005.

[7] Teachings of the Presidents of the Church, page xxviii, quoted in the *Ensign,* January 2005, in "David O. McKay, Ambassador of the Faith."

[8] Gregory A. Prince and Wm. Robert Wright, *David O. McKay and the Rise of Modern Mormonism,* Salt Lake City, University of Utah Press, 2005, page 3.

[9] David O. McKay, "Harmony in the Home," general conference address, Friday, April 6, 1956; published in the Conference Report, April 1956, page 4. https://archive.org/stream/conferencereport1956a#page/n9/mode/1uphttps://www.lds.org/ensign/1985/03/principles?lang=eng.

[10] Richard N. Armstrong, *The Rhetoric of David O. McKay, Mormon Prophet,* New York, Peter Lang Press, 1993, pages 119, 123-124.

[11] *David O. McKay and the Rise of Modern Mormonism,* page 29.

[12] Alma 32:28.

[13] James E. Talmage, *Jesus the Christ*, Salt Lake City, published by The Church of Jesus Christ of Latter-day Saints, 1981, pages 140, 141, 151 [including the notes to chapter 11, note number 4].

[14] Talk by John Butler in Parleys 5th Ward sacrament meeting, February 14, 1999.

[15] Whitney L. Clayton, Blog on Family Search, September 9, 2015, "Teach People, Not Lessons, https://familysearch.org/blog/en/elder-clayton-teach-people-lessons/.

[16] Thomas S. Monson, "How to Communicate Effectively," in *The Voice of My Servants: Apostolic Messages on Teaching, Learning, and Scripture*, ed. Scott C. Esplin and Richard Neitzel Holzapfel, Provo, UT: Religious Studies Center, Brigham Young University; Salt Lake City: Deseret Book, 2010), pages 3 to 10, https://rsc.byu.edu/archived/voice-my-servants/how-communicate-effectively.

[17] Brigham Young, *Journal of Discourses*, Volume 4, page 368.

[18] Lucile C. Tate, Boyd K. Packer: *A Watchman on the Tower*, Salt Lake City, Bookcraft, 1995, page 145; taken from an interview with Dr. Steven Smith, February 2, 1990.

[19] Book of Mormon, Mosiah 2:9

[20] Bruce R. McConkie, "The Purifying Power of Gethsemane," April 1985, https://www.lds.org/general-conference/1985/04/the-purifying-power-of-gethsemane?lang=eng.

[21] *Come, Follow Me for Individuals and Families*, New Testament 2019, published by The Church of Jesus Christ of Latter-day Saints, 2019, page 94.

[22] Jeffrey R. Holland, "Things We Have Learned — Together," a speech delivered at Brigham Young University, January 15, 1985.

[23] Ezra Taft Benson, *Teachings of Ezra Taft Benson*, Bookcraft, Salt Lake City, 1988, page 384, based on a speech he gave at a mission presidents' seminar, June 27, 1974.

[24] Joseph Fielding McConkie, *The Bruce R. McConkie Story: Reflections of a Son*, Salt Lake City, Deseret Book, 2003, page 255.

[25] *The Juvenile Instructor*, April 15, 1905.

[26] *The Juvenile Instructor,* April 15, 1905.

[27] Gene R. Cook, *Teaching By The Spirit,* Salt Lake City, Deseret Book, 2000, page 91.

[28] *Journal of Discourses,* 1: 90-91.

[29] Boyd K. Packer, *Teach Ye Diligently,* Salt Lake City, Deseret Book, 1979, page 304

[30] *Teach Ye Diligently,* pages 354-355.

[31] Boyd K. Packer, "Inspiring Music, Worthy Thoughts," delivered in October 1973 general conference; printed in the January 1974 *Ensign,* https://www.lds.org/ensign/1974/01/inspiring-music-worthy-thoughts?lang=eng.

[32] *Juvenile Instructor,* May 1, 1907, volume 42, page 38.

[33] Vaiangina Sikahema, "Our Religious Obligation to be Educated," devotional address at BYU-Hawaii, delivered on January 14, 2020, https://speeches.byuh.edu/devotional/our-religious-obligation-to-be-educated

[34] *Come, Follow Me for Individuals and Families,* New Testament 2019, published by The Church of Jesus Christ of Latter-day Saints, 2019, page 124.

[35] *Come, Follow Me for Individuals and Families,* New Testament 2019, published by The Church of Jesus Christ of Latter-day Saints, 2019, page 148.

[36] *Come, Follow Me for Individuals and Families,* Book of Mormon 2020, published by The Church of Jesus Christ of Latter-day Saints, 2020, page 16.

[37] *Come, Follow Me for Individuals and Families,* Book of Mormon 2020, published by The Church of Jesus Christ of Latter-day Saints, 2020, page 63.

[38] *Teaching in the Savior's Way,* published by The Church of Jesus Christ of Latter-day Saints, 2016, page 5 of print edition, https://www.lds.org/manual/teaching-in-the-saviors-way/introduction-teaching-in-the-saviors-way?lang=eng&clang=ase=.

[39] *Teaching in the Savior's Way,* page 22 of print edition, https://www.lds.org/manual/teaching-in-the-saviors-way/part-3-teach-the-doctrine/use-music-stories-and-art-to-teach-doctrine?lang=eng.

[40] *Teaching in the Savior's Way,* page 31 of print edition, https://www.lds.org/manual/teaching-in-the-saviors-way/part-4-invite-diligent-learning/ask-inspired-questions?lang=eng.

[41] *Spiritual Roots of Human Relations,* page 254.

[42] Bruce C. Hafen, *A Disciple's Life: The Biography of Neal A. Maxwell,* Salt Lake City, Utah, Deseret Book Company, 2002, page xiv.

[43] *Teaching, No Greater Call,* The Church of Jesus Christ, Salt Lake City, 1999, pages vii and 98.

[44] "We Believe in Being True," *Improvement Era,* Sept. 1959, page 647.

[45] Tom Peters, *Thriving on Chaos,* New York, Perennial Library/Harper & Row, 1988, pages 506 and 587.

[46] Thomas J. Peters and Robert H. Waterman, *In Search of Excellence,* New York, Warner Books, 1982, page 61.

[47] News at Princeton, posted December 5, 2011; https://www.princeton.edu/main/news/archive/S32/27/76E76/index.xml?section=featured

[48] WordWrite Communications, posted by Paul Furiga, April 16, 2013; http://www.wordwritepr.com/Blog/bid/114895/The-science-that-proves-the-effectiveness-of-storytelling-in-business.

[49] *In Search of Excellence,* page 62.

[50] Luke 8:39, Mark 5:19.

[51] Acts 14:27.

[52] Mark 5:19.

[53] Gordon B. Hinckley, "Take Not the Name of God in Vain," October 1987 general conference, https://www.lds.org/general-conference/1987/10/take-not-the-name-of-god-in-vain?lang=eng&_r=1.

[54] Church Handbook of Instructions, Book 2: Priesthood and Auxiliary Leaders, The Church of Jesus Christ of Latter-day Saints, Salt Lake City, 1998, page 304.

⁵⁵ *Teaching, No Greater Call,* page 180.

⁵⁶ Bruce R. McConkie, "The How and Why of Faith-Promoting Stories," New Era, July 1978, page 5.

⁵⁷ Training class attended by the author, Intermountain Health Care central office, July 11, 1995.

⁵⁸ Bruce C. Hafen, *A Disciple's Life: The Biography of Neal A. Maxwell,* page xiv.

⁵⁹ Neal A. Maxwell, "But A Few Days," address to Church Educational System educators, September 10, 1982, https://scottwoodward.org/Talks/html/Maxwell,%20Neal%20A/MaxwellNA_ButAFewDays.html; also included in *Teaching in the Savior's Way,* page 15 of print edition.

⁶⁰ *Church News,* April 20, 2013.

⁶¹ Hundreds of locations on the internet.

⁶² *Spiritual Roots of Human Relations,* page 8.

⁶³ Gordon B. Hinckley, "A Charter for Youth," Conference Report, October 1965, page 52.

⁶⁴ Personal conversation with Nathan Y. Jarvis, winter 2005.

⁶⁵ Written testimony by Heather H. Barth, personal collection of the author.

⁶⁶ Henry B. Eyring, "Write Upon My Heart," October 2000 general conference, reprinted in the November 2000 Ensign, page 87, https://www.lds.org/general-conference/2000/10/write-upon-my-heart?lang=eng&_r=1.

⁶⁷ 1 Nephi 19:23.

⁶⁸ Personal conversation with David H. Meek, February 2016.

⁶⁹ Seminar for new mission presidents, June 25, 2012, published in the LDS Church News, July 7, 2012, http://www.ldschurchnewsarchive.com/articles/62513/Seminar-for-mission-presidents--Lord-will-go-before-you.html.

⁷⁰ Jeffrey R. Holland, *Trusting Jesus,* Salt Lake City, Deseret Book, 2003, pages 155-157.

⁷¹ *Teaching By The Spirit,* pages 64, 122-123.

⁷² Richard Lloyd Anderson "How to Read a Parable," September 1974 *Ensign,* https://www.lds.org/ensign/1974/09/how-to-read-a-parable?lang=eng.

⁷³ Boyd K. Packer, "The Candle of the Lord," https://www.lds.org/ensign/1983/01/the-candle-of-the-lord?lang=eng, June 25, 1982.

⁷⁴ "The Wondrous and True Story of Christmas: First Presidency Message," December 2000 Ensign, https://www.lds.org/ensign/2000/12/the-wondrous-and-true-story-of-christmas?lang=eng.

⁷⁵ "'I Have a Dream' Leads Top 100 Speeches of the Century," University of Wisconsin-Madison, December 15, 1999, https://news.wisc.edu/i-have-a-dream-leads-top-100-speeches-of-the-century/

⁷⁶ Bradley R. Wilcox, "Worthiness Is Not Flawlessness," October 2021 general conference, https://abn.churchofjesuschrist.org/study/general-conference/2021/10/35wilcox?lang=eng&adobe_mc_ref=https%3A%2F%2Fwww.churchofjesuschrist.org%2Fstudy%2Fgeneral-conference%2F2021%2F10%2F35wilcox%3Flang%3Deng&adobe_mc_sdid=SDID%3D3935D97D6EB994C2-75CE7335C105BC93%7CMCORGID%3D66C5485451E56AAE0A490D45%2540AdobeOrg%7CTS%3D1643157256

⁷⁷ *Jesus the Christ,* "He Spake Many Things Unto them in Parables," pages 295, 297, and 299.

⁷⁸ Scott C. Esplin and Richard Neitzel Holzapfel, T*he Voice of My Servants: Apostolic Messages on Teaching, Learning, and Scripture,* Salt Lake City, Deseret Book, 2010, chapter 1: Thomas S. Monson, "How to Communicate Effectively," https://rsc.byu.edu/archived/voice-my-servants/how-communicate-effectively.

⁷⁹ *Teaching By The Spirit,* page 123.

⁸⁰ *Teaching By The Spirit,* page 125.

⁸¹ David A. Bednar, "Watchful Unto Prayer Continually," October 2019 general conference, https://www.churchofjesuschrist.org/study/general-conference/2019/10/22bednar?lang=eng

⁸² *Spiritual Roots of Human Relations,* pages 51-52.

[83] *Teaching By The Spirit,* page 181.

[84] *Teaching in the Savior's Way,* page 22 of print edition, https://www.lds.org/manual/teaching-in-the-saviors-way/part-3-teach-the-doctrine/use-music-stories-and-art-to-teach-doctrine?lang=eng.

[85] *Sports Illustrated,* "The Evolution of the Left Tackle," September 25, 2006, pages 59 and 60.

[86] L. Tom Perry, "Making the Right Decisions," general conference, October 1979, https://www.lds.org/general-conference/1979/10/making-the-right-decisions?lang=eng.

[87] Blair M. Kent, email sent at Intermountain Medical Center, March 28, 2019.

[88] "The Irresistible Power of Storytelling as a Strategic Business Tool," by Harrison Monarth, Harvard Business Review, March 11, 2014.

[89] Blair M. Kent, email sent at Intermountain Medical Center, January 25, 2019.

[90] Personal conversation with Blair M. Kent, May 21, 2020.

[91] "The Lesson Aim: How to Select It, How to Develop It, How to Apply It," Juvenile Instructor, April 15, 1905, page 242.

[92] *Teach Ye Diligently,* page 71.

[93] *Teaching By the Spirit,* page 124.

[94] *Teaching By The Spirit,* page 123.

[95] M. Russell Ballard, "President Gordon B. Hinckley," *Ensign* magazine, September 1994, page 9.

[96] Email sent by H. Gary Pehrson to the author, December 21, 2009.

[97] AZ Quotes, Wolfgang Amadeus Mozart, http://www.azquotes.com/quote/555629.

[98] "Innovators and Influencers of 2016," *Golf Digest,* April 26, 2016, http://www.golfdigest.com/story/innovators-and-influencers-of-2016.

99 *Come, Follow Me for Individuals and Families,* Book of Mormon 2020, published by The Church of Jesus Christ of Latter-day Saints, 2020, page 76.

100 George R. Hill, "President David O. McKay, Father of the Modern Sunday School, *Instructor,* September 1960, page 313.

101 Conference Report, April 1912, page 52.

102 Church News, "A Treasury of Stories," January 17, 2015.

103 Bruce R. McConkie, *Doctrinal New Testament Commentary,* 3:246–47, Salt Lake City, Deseret Book, 2002.

104 Joseph Smith History, 1:12-13.

105 Dieter F. Uchtdorf, "The Why of Priesthood Service," April 2012 general conference, https://www.lds.org/general-conference/2012/04/the-why-of-priesthood-service?lang=eng.

106 *Come, Follow Me — For Individuals and Families,* published by The Church of Jesus Christ of Latter-day Saints, 2018, page 3 of print edition, https://www.lds.org/study/manual/come-follow-me-for-individuals-and-families-new-testament-2019/01?lang=eng.

107 *Come, Follow Me — For Individuals and Families,* 2019, pages viii and ix of print edition.

108 Benson Bobrick, *Wide as the Waters: The Story of the English Bible and the Revolution It Inspired,* New York, Simon & Schuster, 2001, https://books.google.com/books?id=lvyKnhiavIMC&pg=PT62&dq=quotes,+lancelot+andrewes,+%22left+abandoned%22&hl=en&sa=X&ved=0ahUKEwjxhNz31ZfPAhVGwiYKHRbNAioQ6AEIHjAA#v=onepage&q=quotes%2C%20lancelot%20andrewes%2C%20%22left%20abandoned%22&f=false.

109 Dallin H. Oaks, "Gospel Teaching," October 1999 general conference, https://www.lds.org/general-conference/1999/10/gospel-teaching?lang=eng.

110 Teachings: Joseph Smith, lesson manual, chapter 24: Leading in the Lord's Way, https://www.lds.org/manual/teachings-joseph-smith/chapter-24?lang=eng#3-36481_000_028.

111 *Juvenile Instructor,* May 1, 1907, volume 42, page 38.

[112] "The Lesson Aim: How to Select It, How to Develop It, How to Apply it," *Juvenile Instructor*, April 15, 1905.

[113] *The Instructor,* September 1960, page 314.

[114] *Come, Follow Me for Individuals and Families,* New Testament 2019, published by The Church of Jesus Christ of Latter-day Saints, 2019, page 64.

[115] *Come, Follow Me for Individuals and Families,* New Testament 2019, published by The Church of Jesus Christ of Latter-day Saints, 2019, pages 187-188.

[116] *Come, Follow Me for Individuals and Families,* Book of Mormon 2020, published by The Church of Jesus Christ of Latter-day Saints, 2020, page 64.

[117] *Come, Follow Me for Individuals and Families,* Book of Mormon 2020, published by The Church of Jesus Christ of Latter-day Saints, 2020, page 32.

[118] *Teaching By The Spirit,* page 65.

[119] Conversation with Mark J. Ott, MD, November 2015.

[120] Merlin R. Lybbert, "A Latter-day Samaritan," April 1990 general conference, https://www.lds.org/general-conference/1990/04/a-latter-day-samaritan?lang=eng.

[121] Gordon B. Hinckley, "How to Be a Teacher When Your Role as a Leader Requires You to Teach," General Authority Priesthood Board Meeting, February 5, 1969.

[122] Dallin H. Oaks, "The Challenge to Become," October 2000 general conference, https://www.lds.org/general-conference/2000/10/the-challenge-to-become?lang=eng&_r=1.

[123] Bonnie D. Parkin, "Remember Who You Are!," BYU fireside address, March 7, 2004, https://speeches.byu.edu/talks/bonnie-d-parkin/remember/

[124] Benjamin M. Z. Tai, "The Power of the Book of Mormon in Conversion," April 2020 general conference, https://www.churchofjesuschrist.org/study/general-conference/2020/04/27tai?lang=eng

[125] Thomas S. Monson, "Thou Art a Teacher Come From God," Conference Report, October 1970 general conference, pages 104-108, http://scriptures.byu.edu/gettalk.php?ID=1811.

[126] Russell T. Osguthorpe, "One Step Closer to the Savior," October 2012 general conference, https://www.lds.org/general-conference/2012/10/one-step-closer-to-the-savior?lang=eng.

[127] Marion G. Romney, "First Presidency Message: Principles of Temporal Salvation," April 1981 *Ensign*, https://www.lds.org/ensign/1981/04/principles-of-temporal-salvation?lang=eng.

[128] James H. Bekker, address at Parleys Stake conference, January 11, 2020

[129] Alma 36: 17-21.

[130] *Seven Habits of Highly Effective People*, page 98.

[131] Rosemary M. Wixom, "Discovering the Divinity Within," October 2015 general conference, https://www.lds.org/general-conference/2015/10/discovering-the-divinity-within?lang=eng.

[132] Bruce C. Hafen, *A Disciple's Life*, Salt Lake City, Deseret Book, 2002, page 290.

[133] Michael John U. Teh, "The Power of the Word of God," March 2013 *Ensign*, https://www.lds.org/ensign/2013/03/the-power-of-the-word-of-god?lang=eng.

[134] Bonnie L. Oscarson, "Defenders of the Family Proclamation," General Women's Session, March 28, 2015, https://www.lds.org/general-conference/2015/04/defenders-of-the-family-proclamation?lang=eng.

[135] James O. Mason, "A New Health Missionary Program, October 1971 general conference, https://www.lds.org/ensign/1971/12/a-new-health-missionary-program?lang=eng.

[136] Elaine S. Dalton, "Be Not Moved!", General Young Women's Meeting, March 20, 2013, https://www.lds.org/general-conference/2013/04/be-not-moved?lang=eng.

[137] Quentin L. Cook, "Restoring Morality and Religious Freedom," December 2011 commencement address at BYU-Idaho, September 2012 Ensign, https://www.lds.org/ensign/2012/09/restoring-morality-and-religious-freedom?lang=eng.

[138] *The Bruce R. McConkie Story: Reflections of a Son*, page 9.

[139] Jeffrey R. Holland, "For Times of Trouble," devotional address at BYU, March 18, 1980, https://speeches.byu.edu/talks/jeffrey-r-holland_times-trouble/.

[140] Allen D. Haynie, "Remembering In Whom We Have Trusted, October 2015 general conference, https://www.lds.org/ensign/2015/11/sunday-afternoon-session/remembering-in-whom-we-have-trusted?lang=eng.

[141] Hymns of the Church of Jesus Christ of Latter-day Saints, 1985, page 241.

[142] Thomas S. Monson, "Examples of Righteousness," April 2008 general conference, https://www.lds.org/general-conference/2008/04/examples-of-righteousness?lang=eng&_r=1.

[143] Neal A. Maxwell, "Called and Prepared from the Foundation of the World," April 1986 general conference, https://www.lds.org/general-conference/1986/04/called-and-prepared-from-the-foundation-of-the-world?lang=eng.

[144] Clifton Fadman, *The Little, Brown Book of Anecdotes*, Boston, 1985, page 140.

[145] Dieter F. Uchtdorf, "The Merciful Obtain Mercy," April 2012 general conference, https://www.lds.org/general-conference/2012/04/the-merciful-obtain-mercy?lang=eng.

[146] Teachings of Heber J. Grant, The Church of Jesus Christ of Latter-day Saints, chapter 4; taken from the April 1939 Conference Report, page 18, https://www.lds.org/manual/teachings-heber-j-grant/chapter-4?lang=eng.

[147] Numerous internet references, including GoodReads, http://www.goodreads.com/quotes/162599-according-to-most-studies-people-s-number-one-fear-is-public.

[148] "Speaking in Sacrament Meeting" by John Hilton III and Mindy Raye Friedman, New Era, October 2011, https://abn.churchofjesuschrist.org/study/new-era/2011/10/speaking-in-sacrament-meeting?lang=eng

[149] Reyna I. Aburto, "Thru Cloud and Sunshine, Lord, Abide With Me," October 2019 general conference, https://www.churchofjesuschrist.org/study/general-conference/2019/10/31aburto?lang=eng

[150] "The Power of Vulnerability, http://brenebrown.com/.

[151] Ulisses Soares, "Be Meek and Lowly of Heart," October 2013 general conference, https://www.lds.org/general-conference/2013/10/be-meek-and-lowly-of-heart?lang=eng.

[152] *Teaching By the Spirit*, pages 37-41, 73-74; Moses 6:32.

[153] John 1:39.

[154] *Juvenile Instructor,* May 1, 1907, volume 42, page 38.

[155] "The Lord Closed the Book," *Ensign,* February 2006, https://www.lds.org/ensign/2006/02/the-lord-closed-the-book?lang=eng.

[156] Quoted by Boyd K. Packer in "Teach the Children," *Ensign,* February 2000, https://www.lds.org/ensign/2000/02/teach-the-children?lang=eng.

[157] Conversation with David H. Meek, August 17, 2016.

[158] Tom Peters, *The Pursuit of Wow,* New York, Vintage Books, 1994, pages 288-289.

[159] Bruce R. McConkie, *Mormon Doctrine,* Second Edition, Salt Lake City, Bookcraft, 1966, pages 703-704.

[160] *Teaching By The Spirit,* page 78.

[161] Leon R. Hartshorn, *Outstanding Stories by General Authorities Volume III,* Deseret Book, 1975, page 177; devotional address at Brigham Young University-Idaho by Sheri L. Dew, "True Blue, Through and Through," March 16, 2004; Preparation of Joseph F. Smith, "True Blue, Through and Through," https://www.youtube.com/watch?v=TEKiOH-cIbU.

[162] *Teaching By the Spirit,* page 73, italics added.

[163] Neal A. Maxwell, "Teaching by the Spirit — The Language of Inspiration," CES Symposium on the Old Testament, August 15, 1991, Teaching Seminary Preservice Readings Religion 370, 471, and 475, (2004), 35-40, https://www.lds.org/manual/teaching-seminary-preservice-readings-religion-370-471-and-475/teaching-by-the-spirit-the-language-of-inspiration?lang=eng.

[164] Henry B. Eyring, "Serve with the Spirit," October 2010 general conference, https://www.lds.org/general-conference/2010/10/serve-with-the-spirit?lang=eng&_r=1.

[165] Henry B. Eyring, "Eternal Families," April 2016 general conference, https://www.lds.org/general-conference/2016/04/eternal-families?lang=eng&_r=1.

[166] Jeffrey R. Holland, "The Tongue of Angels," April 2007 general conference, https://www.lds.org/general-conference/2007/04/the-tongue-of-angels?lang=eng&_r=1.

ABOUT THE AUTHOR

Richard Nash is a writer and popular speaker (and sometimes an unpopular one, depending on the topic). He previously worked in management and marketing for Intermountain Healthcare and as a speechwriter and jokewriter for business and political leaders. He's a former bishop in The Church of Jesus Christ of Latter-day Saints.

Richard has written for the Harvard Business Review, The Hill, Southwest Art, the Ensign, and other publications, and his previous book, Lengthen Your Smile, was a bestseller in the 1990s. He's lectured to medical, professional, and community groups on subjects including living well, stress management, health care reform, and humor at work (which should never be an oxymoron). (Unless you're an undertaker.)

Richard and his wife, Laurie, live in Salt Lake City and have three children and four grandchildren.

9 781940 498096